I Hold the Heights

I HOLD
THE HEIGHTS

PETER MULGREW

Doubleday & Company, Inc., Garden City, New York
1965

This book was published under the title *No Place for Men*, through A. H. and A. W. Reed, New Zealand.

Foreword

Peter Mulgrew has often jokingly claimed that his life has
been a constant struggle against greatly-to-be-feared bore-
dom. There is much truth in this. It has shown itself in Peter's
abounding enthusiasm for any project that has any likelihood
of excitement or challenge. This enthusiasm isn't always in-
fluenced by practical possibilities or human limitations (his
own included), but, tempered as it is by the loyalty and reli-
ability engendered by his long service in the Navy, it makes
Peter a very useful man to have on an expedition.

The loss of his feet from the frostbite he incurred at 27,000
feet on Mount Makalu has made no noticeable diminution of
Peter Mulgrew's determination to live his life to the fullest.
His friends have come to recognize the gleam in his eye
which warns that a new idea is brewing—an idea that will
embroil him, likely enough, in another dose of excitement,
discomfort, and danger.

E. P. Hillary

I have not lost the magic of long days;
    I live them, dream them still.
Still am I master of the starry ways,
    And freeman of the hill.
Shattered my glass, ere half the sands had run—
I hold the heights, I hold the heights I won.
            —from *I Hold the Heights*,
             by Geoffrey Winthrop Young

Preface

This book is in no way an official or full account of the Himalayan Scientific and Mountaineering Expedition, 1960–61. The full story of that expedition, led by Sir Edmund Hillary and sponsored by the World Book Encyclopedia, has been recorded in *High in the Thin Cold Air*, by Sir Edmund Hillary and Desmond Doig.

What follows in these pages is a personal record of my travels in the Himalayas, my part in the assault on Makalu, and something of the difficulties that beset me afterward. Inevitably many of my companions and their contributions to the expedition are only briefly mentioned, but this is solely because they were engaged on work or activities different from my own.

I have been fortunate, in my writing, to have had the help of a number of persons closely connected with my own experiences, and to these I express my best thanks.

I wish, in particular, to record my indebtedness to John Harrison for the maps and for the unrestricted use of his diary. Also to Michael Ward for the material in the Appendix, "Medical Aspects."

With few exceptions the bulk of the photographs are from 35-mm. color slides taken either by myself or by Sir Edmund Hillary, John Harrison, Walter Romanes, or Michael Gill, all of whom willingly gave me access to their photographic collections. In this connection special mention must be made of the now historic photograph of the summit of Makalu taken from the air in 1940 by Squadron Leader Cliff Andrews, of Wellington, and made available through John Pascoe, also of Wellington.

It will be obvious to the reader that I owe much to very many people, to some even my life. It is my earnest hope that I have made this abundantly clear in the text and that in so doing I have adequately recorded my gratitude.

On my return from Nepal to the hospital in New Zealand I was assisted in every way possible by the New Zealand Government and personally by the Prime Minister, the Right Honorable K. J. Holyoake, also by the New Zealand Naval Board and various government departments. Later, during my convalescence, I went to the United States of America for medical treatment through the consideration and thoughtfulness of Mr. Marshall Field and Mr. Bailey Howard, both of Chicago. In San Francisco, where my wife and I lived for five months, we were received with very great kindness by General and Mrs. Edwin L. Johnson, Dr. and Mrs. H. Loon, Dr. and Mrs. G. Barnes, and Mr. and Mrs. W. Gibson. To all of these we convey our most grateful thanks.

The book has been written as a partnership by my wife, June, and myself. Its merits, if any, we share; its faults are my responsibility. In its production we have been helped enormously by trenchant criticism, both literary and technical, from various friends, in particular Dr. James Houston of Auckland, John Walton of Blenheim, and Geoffrey Lee-Martin of Auckland. The last-named must bear the unenviable distinction of being the one who first thought of writing it and who, by dint of masterly persuasion, finally managed to set me to work.

Auckland   *Peter Mulgrew*
May, 1964

Contents

Foreword, by Sir Edmund Hillary   *v*

PREFACE   *vii*

LIST OF ILLUSTRATIONS   *xi*

One. *Ways and Means*   *1*

Two. *The Push to Patna*   *5*

Three. *The Hunt for the Snowman*   *28*

Four. *Across the High Pass*   *43*

Five. *The Solu Khumbu: Home of the Sherpa*   *61*

Six. *The Climb Begins*   *80*

Seven. *Advance to the Summit*   *99*

Eight. *Disaster and Retreat*   *115*

Nine. *"Pinished"*   *130*

Ten. *Shanta Bhawan*   *142*

Eleven. *Pethidine Pete*   *156*

Twelve. *Return to New Zealand*   *170*

Thirteen. *Look to the Mountains*   *182*

GLOSSARY   *197*

APPENDIX: *Medical Aspects*   *199*

ROSTER OF THE EXPEDITION   *204*

LIST OF ILLUSTRATIONS

Following Page 84

Peter Mulgrew, Michael Gill, and Pat Barcham
Larry Swan and Marlin Perkins displaying Yeti skin
Bhanu Bannerjee with Nepali porter
Sir Edmund Hillary
John Harrison
Wally Romanes
Michael Ward
Leigh Ortenberger
Tom Nevison
Dawa Thondup
Annulu, Urkein, and Mingma Tsering, expedition sirdars
June Mulgrew with her Sherpas
Dawa Tenzing
A Nepali village on the way to the Everest region
Khunjo Chumbi and wife
Lamas from the Khumjung *gompa*

Following Page 108

Everest region seen from the Tesi Lapcha
Crossing the Tesi Lapcha
Makalu col and summit
Sherpa breakfast at Camp II
Camp V on the col
The climb above Camp V
Camp VI
"Get up and take a few more steps . . ."

Maps by John Harrison

The assault on Makalu   page 84
Mount Makalu: Detail of routes above Camp V   page 101

ONE

Ways and Means

Jack Point: For, look you, there is
humour in all things, and the truest
philosophy is that which teaches us to
find it and to make the most of it.
W. S. Gilbert
The Yeomen of the Guard

"How ABOUT coming back to the Himalayas?" Ed Hillary
suggested almost casually. "There's a useful job you can do
on the expedition and I badly need someone with your experience."

I thought for a moment, but there was really no need. We
both knew how obsessed I was with the desire to return. It
was the first really hot day in August 1963, and everything
seemed to be lying drugged and asleep, soaking up the sun.
Below the house, between the line of green-flecked poplar
trees, the shining sea curved into the coast. Although there
was no wind, a light surf crashed onto the beach beside an
olive-green-shrubbed headland, and near its foot the waves
hissed among the rocks.

A few months ago I had not thought that I should ever
return to the Solu Khumbu and the Sherpas, but now, in his
usual generous fashion, Hillary had suddenly presented me
with the opportunity.

"We won't be doing any climbing, of course," he said, "but
you seem to get about so well on those tin legs of yours that
you might as well do some real work on an expedition for a
change and look after the airfield construction program.

"Besides," he added, "I need another old crock like myself
for company while the young bombs do all the climbing."

The invitation, although vaguely uncomplimentary, was warm and I waxed enthusiastic. "The only problem, though," I said, "is the Navy's reaction, but I expect they'll let me go if I can be spared."

The long-suffering Naval Board may well invoke ten thousand maledictions when yet another request for special leave appears on the board-room table, I thought. But the Navy has never lacked imagination and has, from the arctic to the antarctic, since the days of McClintock and Sir John Franklin, evolved almost a tradition of polar exploration.

One of my earliest memories is the winter snows of the distant Tararua Range north of Wellington. I had not the slightest idea why they attracted me so much but, I determined one day to explore them. By the time I was ready to leave secondary school much of both the Northern and Southern Tararuas had become familiar ground and I spent all my school holidays in them, hunting red deer. They may not be high hills, even by New Zealand standards, but they are rugged, and the forests dense, with the open tussock of the high country frequently deep in snow and swept by bitter southerly winds from the antarctic, two thousand miles away. From the Tararuas came my love of the high hills and from them I graduated to climbing and the Southern Alps of New Zealand.

The outbreak of war with Germany, followed by the Battle of the River Plate, turned my thoughts to joining the Navy, and after the war I was glad to stay on and make a career of the sea. I had found that a smooth passage depended, not on the weather, the food, or the Queen's enemies, but rather upon the quality of the bile in certain chief petty officers' digestive systems. One learns, however, in the Navy to take the rough with the smooth and I enjoyed a life which, if at times frustrating, had numerous compensatory advantages. Through the Navy, I and my possessions were transported to all manner of foreign parts and rarely, when within range of mountains or hills, did I not manage to spend a few days ashore.

Nautical men are generally kindhearted and learn to become very tolerant of other men's faults. Nonetheless sailors do tend to place those whose interests lie slightly out of the ordinary run of "normal naval behavior" as "queer fellows." Twenty years of visiting foreign lands wherein I have habitually staggered ashore laden with ice ax, ropes, and other paraphernalia of the mountains has led shellbacked philistines among my shipmates to place me in a similar unseamanlike category. Even to the school that follows the dictum "If it moves, salute it; if it doesn't, paint it," a mountaineer in the Navy is as much beyond the fringe of ordinary comprehension as the navigating officer who wears his bowler hat on the bridge.

The Navy, with admirable restraint, continued to tolerate my requests for climbing leave in various parts of the world, and doubtless took the view that, given enough rope, I might eventually hang myself. Their opportunity came in 1955, when in a weak moment I applied to join the Trans-Antarctic Expedition and asked the Naval Board for three years' special leave. The board acceded to my request with such alacrity that I had no time to withdraw, and before I knew what was happening I found myself trudging disconsolately toward the South Pole. On the morning of January 4, 1958, I transmitted in Morse code the cryptic word "rhubarb," which informed Scott Base and the world that four of us, with Sir Edmund Hillary, had reached the South Pole overland.

The antarctic cemented a close friendship with Hillary and led to an invitation to join his Himalayan Scientific and Mountaineering Expedition.

This time the Navy tempered its forbearance with a certain amount of cut and thrust, but in the end, slightly dazed, generously granted me a full year's leave on half pay.

In order to carry out effectively the major function of the

expedition (physiological research into high-altitude acclimatization) it was necessary to climb, without oxygen, up to or
above 27,500 feet.

At first Hillary hoped to obtain permission to climb Everest again, this time from the north, through Chinese-occupied
Tibet, but after a long delay Peking advised that a permit
would not be granted. He then applied to the Nepalese Government for permission to attempt Makalu, 27,790 feet. The
mountain had already been climbed by the French in the
spring of 1955 under the leadership of M. Jean Franco. With
probably the finest group of climbers ever assembled in the
Himalayas and using large supplies of oxygen, they worked
their way steadily up the mountain. They were favored with
an extraordinary period of fine weather and carried on to
achieve a unique success—all nine members of the assault
party ultimately reached the summit during an assault period
of three days.

To our intense relief the permit arrived, and near the
end of August 1960 we left New Zealand for India.

TWO

The Push to Patna

Still the world is wondrous large,—seven seas from
   marge to marge—
And it holds a vast of various kinds of men;
And the wildest dreams of Kew are the facts of
   Kathmandu,
And the crimes of Clapham chaste in Martaban.

Rudyard Kipling

THE TALL MAN in an outercasing of old jerseys leaped onto
the first vehicle's running board, and with a flamboyant
wave of his arm motioned the others to follow. Obediently
the six heavily laden, brightly painted Mercedes trucks
swung, like a wagon train of the Old West, through the
godown gates and on to the Grand Trunk road toward
Patna, almost four hundred miles away.

Like the Duke of Plaza-Toro, Bhanu and I led from behind, taking our seats in the last truck. There was good reason for this. With thousands of pounds' worth of expedition
equipment in each truck I was anxious to retain some measure
of control, and I planned where possible to run them in con-
voy. As an added precaution I kept the customs papers of
each vehicle with me, so that, should any enthusiast get too
far ahead, he would be held up at successive police check
posts until I arrived with the clearance papers. Smugly satisfied with my masterly organizational ability, I stood modestly
by while Bhanu translated these instructions to the Hindu and
Sikh drivers.

Clearly impressed, they listened with rapt attention, frequently nodding to show approval and murmuring, "*Tikh-
hai, sahib, tikh-hai.*" So much for careful planning. With the

exception of the one that collapsed in the middle of the road
when its wheels fell off, I saw no sign of the remaining trucks
until arrival in Patna thirty-two hours later.

How they got through the check posts without papers remained a mystery, but in any case the police concentrated
their delaying tactics on me, the only one with papers, to
such an extent that I knew we would arrive in Patna four
hours after the last truck was due home. The driver added to
my deepening sense of frustration by insisting on visiting
various relatives en route, all of whom availed themselves of
the opportunity for a free ride to the capital of Bihar Province, plastering themselves all over the truck like currants on
a bun.

My organization having crashed about my ears, I resolved
to adopt a philosophical attitude and redirect the shattered
remnants of the expedition on arrival at Patna. For all I
knew most of the time, I was now responsible for five trucks
fleeing rapidly across the length and breadth of India. I envisaged a warm welcome from Hillary when he found that
I had lost his expedition before it even got as far as Katmandu. Bhanu, my Indian companion, also felt his position
keenly. From the moment we started, our driver had ignored
all Bhanu's instructions and imprecations with a resolution
that, had it been applied to our transit, would have seen us
in Patna with the speed of a racing car.

Being a good Hindu, Bhanu comforted himself with the
thought that merit is not gained without suffering, and the
greater the suffering in this world, the greater reward in the
next. I was pleased to note that although we were now
practically alone on the plains of India he retained a touching faith in my management and rather tended to blame our
misfortunes on the devious qualities of the driver.

Bhanu Bannerjee was employed as assistant to Desmond
Doig, a talented, Nepali-speaking English reporter on the
Calcutta *Statesman*, who had obtained leave of absence to
join the expedition. Like most seamen periodically visiting

Eastern ports, I adhered firmly to the belief that I was a profound orientalist and a fluent speaker of Hindustani. However, since my last visit the indigenous population of Calcutta must have changed, for I found it quite impossible to make myself understood. Rather than reduce myself to the indignity of a sign language, I asked Desmond to let Bhanu accompany me to Patna as interpreter. As well I did, for he proved invaluable and, by making himself useful to the expedition in many ways, ended up by coming right through to Nepal with us.

Bhanu was an excitable, well-educated, high-caste Bengali who, at the time I first knew him, had a compelling desire to emigrate. Like many before him he had written to the American immigration authorities who replied saying that, if he could prove that he was not a madman, a communist, or a person coming to the United States to engage in un-American activities, he might get into America in about fifty years' time. This convinced him that his only hope lay with the British, who seemed inclined to welcome anyone who was not over ninety and did not come from the British Commonwealth of Nations. Bhanu felt that a close association with the expedition and Sir Edmund Hillary might be his key to foreign travel, and he assiduously cultivated those who would further his ambition.

In fairness it must be pointed out that his desire to leave India had nothing to do with frontier problems or Chinese aggression. Had this been so he could simply have joined the Indian Navy, which at the time of the "troubles" is reported to have put up timely posters reading "The Chinese Are at the Gate, Rise to the Occasion. Join the Navy and see Australia."

So far I had met only one or two expedition members, but I knew that by now the others would be gathering in Katmandu, probably at the Royal Hotel where we had block bookings and where, according to rumor, there was a well-stocked bar, the only one in Nepal. I could not hope to reach

Katmandu myself for at least another five days, as I had been
delegated to stay at Patna until the last of the stores were
airlifted over the foothills. We estimated that at least eight
flights would be needed. There is a motorable road all the
way to Katmandu, built by Indian Army sappers, but the
Calcutta trucking company had an attack of the horrors
when we suggested driving the stores right through. Negotiating the road the following year, I felt some sympathy for
their viewpoint, as in parts it is indescribably bad. It crosses
the Terai, a fever-ridden strip of jungle running the length
of the Himalayas and providing some of the finest game
shooting in the world. From Bhimpedi in the foothills the
road then climbs to an altitude of over eight thousand feet
as it winds its way over incredibly difficult terrain toward
Katmandu. The rewards of such a journey, given good
weather, are fantastic views of the distant Himalayas and
glorious photographic opportunities, but on the debit side
must be placed costly road tolls, boiling radiators, and,
for the older car, a one-way trip.

Dusk had long since fallen as we passed the outskirts of
Calcutta. We drove through the night, along roads frequented by bullock carts and by a surprising number of
transport trucks similar to our own. The yoked bullocks
plodded contentedly along the center line of the road, un-
tended and seemingly careless of the noisy passage of modern
India. Their melancholy apathy infuriated our impatient
driver, who launched the truck at them, blowing his horn
and flashing his lights as though engaged in some personal
life-and-death vendetta. These attacks invariably awoke the
teamsters, usually slumbering happily somewhere within the
confines of their carts. This would result in a heated exchange
of Bihari pleasantries, invariably to the advantage of our
driver, who, backed and avidly supported by his free-load-
ing relatives, could easily have outshouted a whole regiment
of the most voluble bullock drivers.

We drove on through the heat of the next day, passing

large areas of sparsely inhabited, rough-looking scrub jungle that was obviously all the driver claimed ("Good tiger country, sahib"). With awful relish he told us that less than a week before a young woman had been killed by a tiger within fifty yards of the road. A passenger in a bus stranded with a flat tire, she sought the seclusion of some nearby bushes and had been taken by the tiger within sight of her husband and children.

In the late afternoon we reached the first police check post. The attending corporal disclaimed all knowledge of the other trucks, although I guessed that he had let them through. It was obvious that papers represented no problem to drivers prepared for bribery, and the few rupees needed to bribe a mere corporal were as nothing to the sums collected from unofficial passengers. Our stops were regular and usually for the purposes of refreshment. Tea vendors could be found near every village, and our driver would rarely pass one by without pausing to purchase a sticky bun or a cup of dark brown fluid, evidently arrived at by a secret process of dissolving pennies in warm water.

The next morning before the city was astir we drove into Patna and headed straight for the airport. It seemed deserted. The first gate we came to was securely padlocked. I investigated the watchman's hut, but the only occupant, a tattered-looking rooster, promptly flew out the window—and directly into the driver's cooking pot. After breakfast we drove around the airfield perimeter until we found the main gate. Not surprisingly the remainder of the trucks stood in a neat row beside some palms. Feigning great astonishment at our leisurely progress, the drivers explained that, confused by the darkness, they had hurried on, thinking we were in the lead. I was beyond caring. The important thing was that all our goods were intact, and we now had only to wait for the chartered Dakota.

After hours of delay due to bad weather the aircraft arrived and we prepared the first load. Wally Romanes, who had escorted the truck containing the ammunition, kerosene, and petrol, agreed to accompany the first flight to Katmandu. The weather held fine, although cloudy in the afternoons, and we were able to get away two flights, and on one occasion three, each day. Patna is hot and dry, the baked earth giving off an enervating heat that even invaded the shade and harassed the temperamental but helpful Indian Airlines officials.

Fortunately for us, on the morning of our arrival Romanes and I had contacted Jeremy Jasper, the British representative in Patna. Apart from his outstanding qualities as a host Jeremy assisted the expedition in many ways and kept open house to us all as we passed through Patna. Although I enjoyed the comfort of the residency, I was anxious to move on to Katmandu, where expedition headquarters were set up in the grounds of the Hotel Royal. Meeting the others and talking things over in the civilized comfort of the Royal's bar was something to which I could look forward with pleasure.

The Dakota pilot told me that the grounds of the hotel harbored a milling throng of Sherpas newly arrived from the hills. They were camped under the trees and on the tennis court, where our stores lay in confusion, ready for sorting into sixty-pound loads. At Patna the huge mound of stores stacked neatly on the tarmac dwindled rapidly, until at last there were just enough for a final plane load.

I felt an upsurge of excitement as we rose above the green-forested Terai. Unfortunately the weather was poor and a massed bank of cloud lay along the whole length of the Himalayas, hiding the mountains from view and almost filling the pass, our only entrance to the valley. For a short while it rained heavily and I began to think we might be forced to turn back, but eventually we dropped between the hills toward a cluster of ocher farmhouses and green and gold fields surrounding our destination, the short concrete airstrip outside Katmandu.

An excited crowd of clamoring Sherpas swung back the planes' double doors and began loading a pair of tired, flat-topped trucks drawn up near the edge of the runway.

I advanced my watch to local time, for the Nepalese are so determined to show their independence of India that they keep their clocks ten minutes ahead of Indian time. As the only arrival, I rapidly became the center of attraction for a gathering multitude of deformed beggars, all equally determined to carry my valise. Facing the immediate prospect of being torn to pieces, I shouldered my bag and made a dash for the grinning driver of an ancient saloon labeled "Hotel Royal."

Beating back the clamorous cloud of mendicants, I climbed into the car, the more forceful Nepalese equivalents of "Bad show, sir," and "Shame" ringing in my ears.

The five-mile drive to the capital of the valley's three cities —Katmandu, Patna, and Bhadgaon—was accomplished in leisurely fashion, giving me plenty of time to look about. Not that the driver lacked dash, nor that the battered car was particularly unwilling. It was simply a case of senile decay on the part of the vehicle and an inability to get past second gear on the part of the driver. The route lay along a single strip of poorly tarred road bounded by picturesque thatch-roofed hamlets and high pink brick walls. Porters with their oval wickerwork baskets slung by fiber belts across their foreheads plodded beside the road, their strong backs and sure step bringing trade in and out of Katmandu, as they and their ancestors had done for centuries. While they ply the traditional tasks that long ago determined their caste, so also does the farmer, beside whose fields they walk. Farming is the basic work of the valley, and the Newars, the people primarily responsible for developing the Nepalese civilization, have been farming the valley since 500 B.C. Lightly built, tan-skinned people, the Newars erected temples in wood and stone and learned to fire bricks for their multistoried homes and medieval defensive walls.

The three cities, once kingdoms at war with one another, have now long since outgrown the walls that were built to defend them. Tier-roofed pagodas and huge Buddhist stupas extended the cities until, although seven miles apart, they were united by more than seven hundred temples and shrines surrounding the center of the valley.

As the cities grew together, so too did the people unite in worship. Few temples remained purely Hindu or purely Buddhist and ultimately a tantric cult developed, claiming adherents among Hindus and Buddhists alike and gradually absorbing the gods of the less ancient Buddhist persuasion.

War came often to Nepal despite its geographic defenses. The major conquerors of the valley were the hardy warlike peoples of the northern hills, the Gurkhas. Although the Newari culture was suppressed by them, it continued to survive and its influence remained so great that Newari is still the most important language spoken in Nepal, and the only one with any literature.

We drove haltingly toward the maidan, a large expanse of level turf used as a parade ground. Regular soldiers in gorgeous scarlet and maroon uniforms marched behind a troop of horse soldiers pulling mountain guns. Gathered around two sides of the grounds, an astonishing variety of the mixed populace looked on, spectacular evidence of the range and density of the numerous ethnic groups composing the 107,000 citizens of Katmandu. Blocked by the crowds, we were forced to drive around the southern side of the maidan, past the main shopping center and past a tall two-hundred-foot "round tower" erected by General Bhim Sen Thapa, Nepal's first prime minister.

There is a story that General Jang Bahadur Rana, a famous Nepalese warrior, once jumped his horse from atop the tower. He not only survived but picked himself up uninjured, although his horse was killed. Nearby we passed a seven-ton equestrian statue of the general, the heaviest single load ever carried into the valley by porters. I was totally unprepared for the magnificent edifice that greeted my eyes as we turned through the tall lodge gates of the Hotel Royal. On the edge of the tennis court, beside the bougainvillaea-flanked drive, Hillary and Norman Hardie supervised the re-packing of a monstrous mound of food and equipment. Sherpas swarmed everywhere, dressed in a motley collection of Tibetan clothing, old jerseys, balaclavas, and sand shoes. Behind them the enormous stuccoed front of the hotel, which had once been the palace of a prime minister, stood almost self-consciously, as though aware of its less exalted station in life. The building had recently been repainted and the words "Hotel Royal" were picked out in electric lights across the width of the former palace. The external wiring of this display was an electrician's nightmare, while its lethal qualities were enhanced by the fact that it utilized so many bulbs the interior of the hotel dimmed to the gloom of an Aladdin's cave whenever the sign was illuminated.

The converted palace retained much of the trappings and splendor of its previous owners. Tasteless furniture of vast dimensions and bygone times filled the rooms, and in the long gallery Rana generals and their ladies, painted in oils and hung in massive gilded frames, loomed menacingly on the walls. The greater-than-life-size portraits were painted in the Edwardian style, and the scarlet uniforms, medals, and gold braid looked out of place here, more befitting an English ancestral home than this remote outpost city.

Inhabited by a few dazed animals, a small private zoo adjoined the hotel, and in the unkempt grounds behind the tennis courts a marble naiad sorrowed over an artificial lake stocked with goldfish. The size of some of the Victorian acquisitions astounded me, considering that everything had to be carried over the mountains on the backs of porters. Greek statuary and pianos had been portered in, and even a Rolls-Royce—regardless of the lack of roads to drive upon.

With Ed Hillary, Norman Hardie, and George Lowe, I shared a large room on an extension of the second floor, above what once had been an audience chamber. A large naval kit bag with "Hillary" roughly painted across it stood in a corner of the room, and two suitcases displayed their contents on one of the four beds. Hillary pecked away at a typewriter beside the single small window, and George Lowe lay sprawled across one of the beds studying a crisp new Royal Geographical map of the Everest region.

It was good to see George again; he had just returned from Greenland with Sir John Hunt, barely in time to leave London for the Himalayas. Born in New Zealand, George capped a distinguished climbing career by playing a major part in the successful British Everest expedition of 1953 and later crossing the Antarctic Continent with Sir Vivian Fuchs.

In what should have been the focal point of the hotel, the "Yak and Yeti" bar, but which was deserted because of a liquor shortage, I found Drs. Larry Swan and Tom Nevison, both from California. Born in India and schooled in Darjeeling, Larry spoke Hindustani well and was attached to the expedition as a biologist. Like Tom Nevison, who had been to the Karakoram with an American expedition, Larry was no stranger to the Himalayas, having collected specimens in the Barun Valley with the Californian Makalu expedition.

We were joined in the bar by the bulk of the expedition's climbing contingent, Dr. Jim Milledge, of the United Kingdom, and three highly successful young New Zealand climbers, Pat Barcham, Wally Romanes, and Mike Gill. Soon we were submerged in exciting discussions of the Himalayas and Makalu.

With Pat Barcham and Wally Romanes I was kept fully occupied for two days, sorting and issuing expedition equipment from a small room on the ground floor of the hotel. Mine, I found, was the task of fitting each Sherpa with his climbing boots and crampons, an occupation earthier than I had at first supposed. To meet the expedition, the Sherpas had walked out to Katmandu wearing Tibetan felt boots or Chinese-manufactured plimsolls. These they had neither removed nor changed during the journey. Neither had they observed the elementary convention of washing their feet before attending the issue of gratuitous expedition finery. This resulted in a malodorous accompaniment to the proceedings that I found hard to bear, but that the Sherpas, demonstrating the hillman's traditional solidarity, united in ignoring. Caught by their infectious gaiety, I stood at the storeroom door, my face twisted in a frozen welcoming grin, like a cashier waiting for the bank examiners to arrive.

I was glad of the chance to work with the Sherpas, as it gave me the opportunity to get to know and recognize them, no easy task at first, for initially they all looked alike to me. Norman Hardie introduced me to our sirdar, Dawa Tenzing, succinctly described by Desmond Doig as a "patriarchal figure of indeterminate age who exudes personality and alcoholic fumes."

A Sherpa of the old school, D.T., as he was affectionately known, had plaited hair and untidy mandarin whiskers. He exercised enormous authority over the Sherpas and brooked no disobedience or disrespect. Dealing with fractious Sherpas or young sahibs, Dawa had a certain wintry presence that always gave me that "new recruit" feeling. He was very polite, but I suspected that he regarded as brash newcomers all those who had not completed five Himalayan expeditions or at least been above twenty-five thousand feet. He was on Everest with General Bruce in 1924 and since then has developed one of the finest climbing records of any Sherpa and of most Europeans. In 1958 he was the victim of a terrible double tragedy. While he and his son were on separate expeditions, he on Everest, his eldest son on Jugal Himal, rumor reached his wife that both husband and son had been killed in an avalanche. Desolate with grief, she walked down to the river below her village and hurled herself in. When Dawa arrived back at his home village of Khumjung, he heard that his son had indeed been killed and that his wife was dead.

Dawa Tenzing's two deputy sirdars were also experienced

climbers and personally well known to Hillary. Urkein, the more sophisticated of the two, proved exceptionally tough and strong, but somewhat unpredictable through an addiction to *rakshi*, the Sherpas' fiery local brew. Annulu's addiction, no less compelling, seemed to be women—he had been married three times and proudly admitted to seven children.

Each member of the party had a Sherpa appointed to look after his well-being and act as a personal man and climbing companion, a sort of Asiatic gentleman's gentleman. Although gregarious in habit, the Sherpas are decidedly individualistic in appearance, particularly in their choice of dress. Dawa Thondup, my Sherpa, was no exception. He wore, pinned to a bright blue sweater, a small plastic-covered photograph of the Dalai Lama. His oiled hair was plaited in the old style and wound around his head as a topknot, while all this was capped with an ancient red balaclava, a relic of the Japanese Manasalu expedition. His assorted garments gave him a swashbuckling appearance that belied his quiet and sometimes moody manner, but he was generally cheerful and at times his brown eyes simply danced with hidden humor.

Dawa Thondup was such a convinced and ardent Buddhist that on one occasion I saw him purchase fish as a fisherman landed them and throw them back into the river. If I viewed him with interest, Dawa was no less absorbed in me and my belongings, and he quickly made it his business to learn something of my background. He was inordinately proud of his three-year-old son and was once heard to inquire, *sotto voce*, how many sons Peter Sahib had. He wilted somewhat on being told that after tens years of marriage I had but two daughters—and no sons.

At first I was ashamed at my loss of status, but I need never have worried, for it proved only a temporary embarrassment to Dawa, who cheerfully invented sons for me whenever the need arose.

We received word that more than five hundred Nepali porters, gathered from the surrounding countryside, were camped at Banepa ready to carry the loads that were now ready. The need for so many porters arose from the unusually long time we expected to spend in the Himalayas—almost a year—and the consequent major supply problem.

The considerable finance required for such a lengthy expedition came largely from the American publishers of the World Book Encyclopedia, part of the Field Enterprises Educational Corporation. The primary objective of the expedition was physiological research into the acclimatization of the human body at extreme altitudes. In order to carry out the program it was intended to winter a party at a height of about 20,000 feet. After the winter, a mixed group of those who had an opportunity to acclimatize thoroughly through living at high altitudes for some months, plus some fresh, relatively unacclimatized mountaineers, would attempt the ascent of Mount Makalu, 27,790 feet. This attempt was to be made without the use of supplementary climbing oxygen and, if successful, would make Makalu the highest peak thus far scaled without oxygen. The senior scientist, Dr. Griffith Pugh, was physiologist with the successful British Everest expedition of 1953. His work, backed by the British Medical Research Council, was to be an extension of his Everest work, and he would be supported by six other physiologists.

Although wintering at 20,000 feet had not been attempted before, it was not expected to offer problems greater than those of logistics, that is, getting the necessary food, fuel, and shelter to such a height. A carefully controlled program of acclimatization was planned and modern methods and equipment to record the performance of various climbers would be used. The most interesting of these to me was the proposed telemetering system, which would broadcast continuous information on the climber's pulse rate, breathing, step rate, etc. The information, on tape or transmitted by radio, would be received and analyzed by the scientists at lower altitudes, whose mental functions should be comparatively unimpaired by anoxia. With a camp occupied during the winter months

there existed a unique opportunity for original meteorological
and glaciological research, as well as exploration and map-
ping, and as I expected, Hillary and Pugh intended to take
full advantage of it.

Of less importance, but possibly of more stimulus to the
imagination, was the main activity of the first four months
of the expedition, when a serious attempt was to be made to
unravel mysteries that seemed to hint at fact rather than fable.
Hiding away in his mountain fastnesses the legendary Yeti
(Snowman) would need to keep on the move if he hoped to
remain a mystery, for Hillary intended us to search the
length of the Rolwaling Valley near the Tibetan border for
signs of him. Belief in the existence of the creature is based
largely on the evidence of tracks that have been discovered
on many isolated snow fields in the Himalayas. Some of these
tracks resemble those of bears or snow leopards, but many
show characteristics that are quite unusual and indicate a
creature of considerable weight, walking upright on two legs,
and with feet similar to those of a large and abnormally
broad human. The inhabitants of the Himalayas are firmly
convinced of the existence of the Yeti, and although much
of their belief could be written off as superstition some of
their stories were obviously worth fuller investigation.

The Snowman, should he appear, was not to be callously
slaughtered, but would be immobilized for closer examination by means of air guns firing hypodermic syringes
and loaded with knock-down drugs. Photographed, finger-
printed, and measured, swabbed and brain-washed, our Yeti
would then be free to stagger back to the freedom of the
mountains—"with nothing worse than a puzzled look in
front and a dab of iodine behind," as a newspaper editor so
aptly remarked.

Hillary planned to spend about a month in the Rolwaling
Valley and, if no positive evidence were discovered, then to
transfer the search to the Dudh Kosi near Everest. He expected conditions to become more rigorous as winter ap-

proached, but this should prove the ideal time to locate the Yeti, as the creature is supposedly driven to lower pastures by the cold winter snows. The expedition, then, was to be divided into several activities during three main periods. During the first period, of about four months of 1960, the majority of the party would assist in the search for the Yeti. Various lookout camps would be established at heights of 17,500 feet to 18,500 feet and a careful watch kept from these. Men in the lookout camp would be periodically relieved and opportunities given for a more active period of climbing and exploration.

Meanwhile a small group under Norman Hardie would conduct the main body of coolies with all the supplies into the Everest region and depot them at Thyangboche. They would then enter the Mingbo Valley and construct a hut at 17,000 feet (known as the Green Hut), later combining with the Rolwaling party to build the wintering hut near the Ama Dablam Col.

The second period, covering January to March 1961, would see the winter party established and the physiological program started, which would be continued till the end of May. The third and final period, April and May 1961, would be devoted to the establishing of the route on Makalu and the final assault, without oxygen.

On September 13, 1960, the first of the two groups of the expedition started from Katmandu: Hardie, with 320 laden porters, began the seventeen-day march to Thyangboche. A day later Hillary, with 150 porters, set out for the Sherpa village of Beding, close by the Tibetan border. Everyone was happy and delighted to be actually on the way at last, that is, everyone except me. I was still in Katmandu suffering from an unpleasant bout of amoebic dysentery, probably contracted in India. I was furious although in no condition to argue about remaining behind, as having dysentery is a full-time occupation. I recovered after a few days, but I had to organize my own bundobust and hurry after Hillary, by now nearing the Rolwaling Valley and over a hundred miles away.

Apart from Dawa Thondup and myself, Bhanu was also absent when the expedition departed. He had returned to Calcutta in quest of some delayed stores items, but I had expected him back in time to accompany us, and indeed I looked forward to his early arrival. I was, as usual, embroiled in language difficulties.

To overcome this problem, I contacted Narendra Saksena, the *Times* representative in Katmandu and Desmond Doig's colleague. Saksena, an ex-Indian Army Signals officer, proved immensely helpful and immediately set about arranging porters and the hire of a truck to transport us to our starting point at Banepa, fifteen miles from Katmandu. Large-scale expeditions inevitably exert a considerable drain on the available porter community, and Saksena had some difficulty finding enough applicants to meet my modest requirements. Eventually, the evening before we hoped to depart, six roguish-looking Nepali coolies were produced at the hotel room for my inspection.

There was really small point in the interview anyway, as they were probably the only porters looking for work at that moment in the whole Katmandu Valley, and, as they well knew, their acceptance was practically a matter of form. They adopted a devil-may-care attitude, and their leader, a diminutive but pleasant fellow, assured the world at large that the sahib was generosity itself and would undoubtedly provide them all with extra smokes and baksheesh should they make a fast journey.

I had, in fact, said nothing about this possibility, but, as Saksena seemed to regard their arrival in a light similar to that in which Marshal Foch viewed the arrival of the Angels of Mons, I was prepared to agree to almost any fictitious promise, no matter how wild. The leader of the porters was small, even by Nepali standards, and with his unusually high-pitched voice he reminded me of Winnie the Pooh's friend

Piglet. As I could neither remember nor pronounce their names, Piglet and his friends became known collectively as the Vestal Virgins, while for purposes of payment and record I gave each of them a number. The pecuniary details settled to everybody's satisfaction, the Virgins descended on me in a body, like the great potato blight. They would, they said, be delighted to spend the night in my hotel room, so that we may all enjoy an early start the following morning. I was certainly keen to leave, but not that keen, and viewed the proposal with such a singular lack of enthusiasm that Piglet took the hint and, gathering his followers about him, departed. He was graciousness itself. Buoyed by Piglet's protestations of good will and faithful service, I slept well that night, my impatience subsiding as I thought of a fast trip and an early return to the body of the expedition.

The road to Banepa looks like an incredibly rough semi-watercourse, which indeed it is. Fortunately it is motorable, although only barely, and for that I was profoundly thankful. I had no particular desire to walk the first torrid fifteen miles of a two-hundred-mile journey. Saksena had ordered the lorry for 6 A.M. in the hope that it would arrive by 7:30. By 8:30 there were signs of neither the transport nor the porters.

I sent Dawa Thondup off on a winkling-out mission, as I suspected that the Vestal Virgins were simply indulging in a little light decadence and would soon be found in the vicinity of the nearest chang shop.

Katmandu lorries are not in what one would call the first flush of youth, and I had learned from bitter experience with their Indian counterparts not to expect too much of them. But the lorry that pulled into the hotel drive shortly after Dawa Thondup left was worse than any I had seen during the push to Patna. It came staggering and blowing toward the hotel entrance with the desperation of an elderly anarchist about to throw his last bomb. As it drew near us the driver shouted wildly, his ancient bulb horn braying to attract our attention. He had no need to worry; the rapid disintegration of the truck's greaseless bearings might have been heard in Calcutta, and I had not the slightest doubt that even if it did manage to reach Banepa it stood only the slimmest chance of ever getting back. Hard on the tail of the wreck came the porters, in very much better condition than I expected. My hopes rose as Bhanu, who had to my great relief arrived back from Calcutta, got things moving and the truck loaded with speed and enthusiasm.

Our engine shuddering and horn honking, we drove, enveloped in dust, toward Bhadgaon, the ancient capital of the valley. Once through the cobbled streets and ornate square the track quickly became more undulating and rough, with boulders and a profusion of small stones scattered across the way.

On the hills our driver favored a direct frontal assault. Throwing caution to the winds, he dashed at a furious pace down one side of a dip to rise, with a clashing of gears, majestically up the other, a cork on a rough sea. Past hamlets set in a Japanese print landscape of rice paddies and rust-brown fields we drove, our radiator spouting like an enraged whale and our chassis rattling and squeaking in agonized accompaniment to the porters' Nepali singing.

In Banepa's ruined square we regrouped and set off up a gentle slope between tiled houses and gilded temples, surrounded by a ragged following of small boys chattering over proffered sweets. Guided by Piglet, who claimed to have visited the Rolwaling Valley three years earlier, we trudged serpent-like along the narrow stony path toward Hukse, our stopping place for the night. We slept beneath a sacred pipal tree, our brightly colored two-man tent attracting a large part of the local populace, who watched our evening preparations with interest.

In the usual manner of Himalayan travel we began each day at 5:30 A.M. with only a cup of tea. By six our tents were down and the first of the Vestal Virgins would be disappearing along the dry red path, his bare feet kicking up spurts of dust as he walked. The fresh clean mornings were the best, and I often felt a surge of joy at my good fortune, walking freely as the first tepid rays of the sun lit the valley. After a few hours we would make a prolonged halt for breakfast beside some stream or small brook. The track led us eastward, parallel to the chain of mountains forming the Himalayan watershed, and although each day we dropped down into deep valleys and across foaming torrents the climb up the far side increased our hold on the country just a little more.

The distant peaks became sharper and less unreal. The terraced fields gave way to rhododendron and pine forests, with the thatch-roofed houses replaced by those with wooden slat roofs, held down by large flat stones.

Along the track we passed other travelers, usually heading toward Katmandu with huge, laden baskets of produce for the markets. Scantily attired, thin brown men and colorfully dressed girls with flower-like golden nose rings, they all carried loads, usually surmounted by a few scraggy chickens, legs tied and squawking unhappily at their wretched lot.

Compared with the squalid houses near Katmandu, the country villages, particularly struck us with their cleanliness, and certainly their inhabitants looked healthier, although it is fair to add they were for the most part goats.

We made good progress and the porters kept to their word, making between twelve and fifteen miles each day. With sixty-pound loads this was good going and I promised extra rupees all around when we reached Beding. At times we were troubled by Piglet, whose enormous capacity and uncanny ability to locate chang had an unsettling effect on the rest of the Virgins, who were easily led astray. But if at times unsteady, our progress was at least reasonably regular.

On the third day camp was pitched on a grassy patch beside the Risingo Monastery, perched on a forested spur above the river. A Buddhist monk from the monastery approached asking Dawa Thondup if the sahib had pills for a severe headache. It was not his headache he explained, but that of an important lama, a nine-year-old reincarnation at present visiting the monastery. I expressed surprise and said that I had always thought that lamas were obdurate in the face of suffering. The monk agreed that this was usually so, but as the boy had not yet completed his lengthy training he could not be expected to be as resolute in the face of great pain as he undoubtedly would be in the future. After visiting the lama I suspected that there was far more than just a headache involved; however, with no medical knowledge, there was little I could do except content myself by leaving him a small supply of codeine tablets.

At Charikot we turned north, away from the main Everest route, and followed the Bhote Kosi River, directly toward Menlungtse, the 23,500-foot peak of the Gauri Sankar range. The next morning as we crossed the banks of the Gumbu Khola, I just missed treading on a pit viper. Dawa Thondup, a few paces ahead, suddenly leaped into the air and, side-stepping, called me to beware. Hurrying and slithering down the track, a poisonous pit viper passed within a foot of both of us and disappeared down a dry watercourse toward the river. I noticed Dawa carrying a heavy stick for several days after that.

I was surprised that so many people, more than two hundred, could pass through the country ahead of me without apparently leaving any sign of their passage. Even when I came across expedition campsites I found absolutely nothing, not a tin, a fragment of paper, or a spent match, so avidly did the locals collect everything left behind.

As an aid to progress, each morning at breakfast Dawa Thondup fried *puris*, which we all carried in our pockets or down our shirt fronts and ate as we marched. *Puris* are thick pancakes of flour and water, fried and served with chilies. They were normally edible and, I suppose, nourishing when they were hot and eaten with sweet tea, but fished, cold, out of Dawa's grubby pocket, they were not only tasteless but downright impossible to chew. To avoid offense, I usually waited until Dawa was out of sight, then tossed his offering behind a rock, where no doubt they remain as imperishable evidence of my passage.

For the last three days the country was wild, the forests dense, and the mountains reared above us as far as we could see. Cliffs of damp vegetation hung above our heads, and a narrow gorge directed our steps toward a bridge across the Rolwaling Khola. In this area of heavy bush and thick undergrowth we encountered large numbers of leeches, but they were a nuisance rather than a hazard. The porters' bare feet and legs were fair game, and before long they ran blood where the leeches could be seen clustered on their legs, swelling to twice normal size before dropping off.

We crossed to Simigaon, a mean village, high on the opposite bank of the Rolwaling. I was impressed with the bridge, a particularly fine specimen of Tibetan cantilever construction. Masses of beams and tree trunks were arranged in layers, one on top of the other, and lashed together by fiber ropes. Each layer jutted out by about three feet from the layer below it, so that the abutment extended progressively until it met an enormous rock in midstream. A repetition of the formula extended from the opposite bank, forming a crude double arch. The whole structure shook with the force of the water below it and a perpetual mist enveloped the rock, planted squarely in the midst of the torrent.

On the cliffs and in the trees above the bridge a family of Himalayan langur monkeys cavorted, their flat black faces and bosun-type whiskers peering at us as we tackled the steep ascent to Simigaon. We paused briefly at the village for tea and *puris*, but it was a miserable place and I was thankful to move on. The track climbed relentlessly through thick forest, and as the altitude increased Piglet complained that the cold was too much for the porters, who were barefoot and dressed in ragged cotton clothes. I was worried about their accommodation overnight. The weather had worsened and I knew we were going to have heavy rain. I had persuaded them to push on past Simiagon, the last shelter they could expect before Beding, and it was obviously up to me to take care of them. We were all making hard work of the climb, the porters were gasping and panting like winded beagles. I could see that we would not get over the 14,000-foot pass before dark; therefore, the sensible thing to do was camp and complete the evening meal before the clouds broke and the rain swamped us. We were only just in time. The storm burst across the ridge like a whip, scattering the trees and drowning the landscape in a freezing torrent of water. We crowded into the tiny tents, waiting miserably for dawn to come and hoping fervently that the rain might at least ease for our last few hours walk to Beding the next day.

A warm fug, laced with garlic—the porters' seasonal delicacy—invaded the tent and I momentarily regretted my hospitality. Crushed into a corner with Piglet's muddy feet in my face, I slept fitfully on my rock-hard air mattress. Dawa Thondup, who normally blew up my Lilo, had farmed out some of the work, and Piglet, who maintained a sort of proprietary interest in me, had taken Dawa's instructions literally and blown the Lilo to the consistency of an iron slab.

At about two in the morning I could stand the agony no longer and, intending to release some air from the mattress, removed the rubber bung, receiving full in the face a blast of Piglet's garlic-laden breath. This I record as the most nauseating among my more unpleasant experiences.

Next morning we packed our sodden tent in the pouring rain, caring little, for we knew we should not have to sleep in it another night. We toiled toward the pass, slipping in the wet frozen mud, and I for one hoping that the rain might lift long enough for a close-up glimpse of the mountains.

Twice that morning we heard the roar of avalanches from Gauri Sankar, only a narrow valley away, but the peak

itself remained hidden in the driving rain. On the far side of
the pass we began to drop down and the path became steep
and rough, with long slippery stretches where the way ran
through dense woods. After an hour the rain eased and finally ceased, leaving a gray mist rising from the rotting leaves
as a hot midday sun drove through the trees, warming the
shivering, hurrying Virgins.

In a clearing above the river we saw the valley. It was a
beautiful place, but terribly dominated by the fine-propor-
tioned twin peaks of Gauri Sankar. The southern face
plunged sheer down in an awe-inspiring wall of fluted ice
and brooding overhangs, a monolith of rock and fringed
cornices towering above the insignificant village of Beding.

The Hunt for the Snowman

But Scientists, who ought to know,
Assure us that they must be so . . .
Oh! Let us never, never doubt
What nobody is sure about!

"The Microbe"
Hilaire Belloc

"IF FINGERPRINTS CAN HANG A MAN, as they frequently do, surely footprints may be allowed to establish the identity of one." These words of H. W. Tilman referred to the tracks of the Yeti, or, more popularly, the Abominable Snowman, and it was the search for the same tracks and the hope of sighting a Snowman that had brought us into the Rolwaling Valley. The Rolwaling, literally "As Straight as a Potato Furrow," and as deep and unfrequented as any remote Himalayan valley, supports about two hundred people living in three villages. The highest village, Na, near the head of the valley at 14,000 feet, is occupied only during the summer, while Beding, at 12,000 feet, and Chimi Kotchi, at 9000 feet, are winter quarters. The principal monastery and bulk of the people were midway up the valley at Beding, where we had our base camp.

To many of the local people only the God-fearing ever see the elusive Snowman. If one takes no alcohol, smokes no cigarettes, and avoids evil thoughts, the chances of a sighting are immeasurably improved, a combination of requirements altogether too much for our expedition members, none of whom seemed able to qualify on any count. In any case, as the head lama pointed out, we smelled wrong for a Yeti and would only succeed in driving him away if one should be sufficiently inopportune to find himself downwind of us. Bearing the lama's advice in mind, we worked steadily on this particular facet of acceptance by the Snowman, and after a few days of unwashed living would have qualified unconditionally for membership of a compost society anywhere in the world.

Desmond Doig quickly won the affection and respect of the local inhabitants, as much as he already had of the expedition Sherpas. He was exceptionally gentle with them and I never saw him lose his temper, no matter how exasperating the situation. He remained immensely popular with the Nepalese peoples that the expedition contacted throughout Nepal, and it was due to him that we owed much of the Yeti information gathered during our ten months in that country.

It seems there are two main types of Yeti known to the Sherpas. The *dzu-teh*, a large beast up to eight feet in height with long, shaggy hair of a gingery color, said to kill yaks and cattle but generally considered a vegetarian and so harmless to men. The second, the *mih-teh* is the one most often referred to by the Sherpas and is the one in which we were more interested. An unpleasant fellow, not averse to eating humans, he is about five feet tall, walks upright, has a strikingly pointed skull, and is covered with light reddish hair. During the winter, when the heavy snow drives it lower than usual, the *mih-teh* is often heard at night close by the villages. Near at hand it makes a chattering sound but is generally distinguished by its loud wailing, yelping call, which terrifies those within earshot.

Although none of the Sherpas or lamas we met would own to having actually seen a *mih-teh*, several claimed to have seen their tracks and heard them during the colder months higher up the valley. That the Sherpas believe absolutely in the existence of the Yeti there is no doubt, and on the whole their various stories agree in the principal details, but most tales of meetings with Yetis are secondhand and suffer from embellishment in the telling, a liberty not entirely unknown to the more sophisticated Western raconteur.

During the stay in the Rolwaling Valley one of our Sherpas located an aged nun said to possess a genuine Yeti skin. The Yeti had been killed many years previously in Tibet and the skin brought over the border to the Beding Monastery and was now in the home of the nun and her husband, a lama who was at present away on a journey. We were all very anxious to see the skin, but whenever our Sherpa, Ang Temba, suggested a showing he met only a determined refusal. After some days of negotiation Desmond was able to get a look at the skin and reported that it was probably taken from the very rare Tibetan blue bear and well worth purchasing, if the nun could be persuaded to part with it. The British Museum had some blue-bear skins collected by the Younghusband expedition, but as far as was known no European had ever seen one alive. Desmond and Ang Temba worked away on the problem for some time, gradually increasing the pile of proffered rupees. At last the old woman could stand the sight of untold wealth no longer, and, fearful that her husband would return and not only beat her but, worse, refuse to sell the skin, she capitulated and it became ours. It proved a fine specimen, causing great excitement among our Sherpas, who instantly recognized it as the skin of the large *dzu-teh* and no bear at all. Later in the village of Khumjung, many miles away from the Rolwaling Valley, Desmond and Marlin Perkins, director of Chicago's Lincoln Park Zoo, produced the skin for the benefit of several dozen people gathered about our camp and obtained the same interesting reaction. They all regarded it as the skin of the Yeti, and some were quite frightened of it, thinking that just sighting it would probably bring them bad luck.

Apart from photographing it, there were various suggestions on how to capture the Yeti, ranging from digging a pit for the unsuspecting beast, into which we hoped one might stumble, to Rana, the Nepali liaison officer, who offered the

surprisingly witty idea that George Lowe Sahib might offer
to marry one. The most thought-provoking idea, however,
came from Marlin Perkins, whose principal task and ambition
was to lay the Yeti, male or female, by the heels.

He had brought with him from the United States a couple
of "Capshur" guns, which operated much like an ordinary
rifle except that it was a long-range injection needle that
would render the animal, if animal it were, unconscious. Marlin explained with eloquence and enthusiasm how all one had
to do on coming face to face with a Yeti was to estimate
the body weight of the creature, carry out a small mental
calculation, enabling one to set the correct amount of drug
so as not to kill the beast, load the gun, and fire. He had no
need to state the obvious, that, were we to put too little
narcotic in the gun, the animal would in all probability kill
us. In view of the current opinion among the local populace
that the Yeti ate men and stood seven feet high, Marlin's
somewhat remarkable *modus operandi* was justifiably received with screams of laughter from the intrepid Yeti
hunters. In any event I found myself quite unable to do the
mental sum required and, on the one occasion when I did
manage it, took a full six minutes.

The thought of a possible mental aberration, while an enraged Yeti chewed its way through the would-be Nimrod's
arm, must have proved too much for the expedition members,
for I never saw the "Capshur" guns out of their cases.

The country around our camp and a mile or so up the
river was steeply and heavily wooded. The trees grew
thickly from the water's edge for several hundred feet up
the almost precipitous valley sides, thinning out to straggly
patches of stunted growth amid numbers of large rock caves,
which in some instances burrowed back into the hillsides for
fifty feet or so. The view was generally held that any Yeti
with half an ounce of common sense would be a fool if he
did not take up his abode in one of these caves, especially
as many of them were dry and very difficult of access. It

was therefore decided that, before moving on to higher country, as was now Hillary's intention, we should search as many
of the caves as possible in the hope of flushing out a covey
of Yeti.

The suggestion was greeted with acclaim until somebody
pointed out that where there were caves there were probably
bears, and that, generally speaking, the Himalayan brown
variety does not take kindly to an invasion of privacy, however well meaning the intruder and however voluble his protestations that he is only inquiring for Yeti.

Eventually a plan was concocted whereby we would
search in pairs, the fleet of foot to enter the cave, while his
more lumbering companion waited outside with a high-
powered rifle. There was a certain vulpine cunning about the
plan, as, whatever the outcome, someone was bound to get
a surprise. I, however, as one of the supposedly fleet of foot,
found a lack of finesse about the whole idea and had visions
of my breathless arrival at the mouth of the cave, closely
followed by an unfriendly carnivore, either to find my companion fled the field or to receive a blast of buckshot full
in the face.

I communicated my lack of resolution to Marlin, who was
quite unperturbed and suggested a simple solution. I would
carry with me into the cave a tear-gas pencil: as soon as I
met a bear I should discharge the pencil into his face, there-
upon temporarily changing his mind about dinner, giving me
time to dash madly from the cave and the hunter waiting at
the entrance a chance to steel himself, ready to deliver the
coup de grâce to a now thoroughly demoralized bear.

For all Marlin's rather exotic ideas and our brave preparations, it is perhaps fortunate that we never at any time saw
an animal larger than a deer, much less a bear. However, the
danger was real, as there had been several instances in the
valley of native hunters being caught and mauled by bears.
Later in Katmandu, Dr. Jimmy Dick, of the United Mission
Hospital, told me that he had recently completed a long skin-

grafting operation on a hunter who had investigated a brown bear too closely and had half his face ripped off for his pains.

Other than the small gray rock rabbits, or pikas, most of the animals we could expect to find were nocturnal. In the hope of photographing one of these, a fox or perhaps a wolf, Hillary decided to set up our automatic trip cameras, another example of Marlin's fertile imagination. He had brought several cameras operated by trip wires, with the idea that once we located the elusive Yeti's haunts the cameras could be placed along the route taken by the mating Yeti, thus offering irrefutable evidence of the existence of the Snowman.

It had continued to rain fairly heavily ever since my arrival at Beding. Rivulets of water ran past our tents, and waterfalls mysteriously sprang from clefts in the rock walls far above our heads, cascading down the cliffs, to disappear behind the curtain of green forest spreading up from the camp, cutting muddy channels through the undergrowth and turning the river even grayer as it raced torrentially down the valley toward India.

The rain did not keep away the villagers from Beding Monastery, and they would be found at most times of the day gazing with awe and reverence at the confines of the mess tent, where Mike Gill lay in one corner surrounded by oxygen equipment, slowly recovering from the astonishing and entirely involuntary purple shade he had turned when he had contracted pneumonia a few days previously. In the other corner John Dienhart, who had joined us as a representative of Field Enterprises, waved his arms in ecstasy before the portable radio, tuned to some obscure Indian radio station playing the latest in jazz fashions by an even more obscure Indian band. The villagers were no doubt convinced that the bearded Lama Sahib, muttering incantations and making wild cabalistic signs over the prostrate Gill, was conducting a ritual equaled only by their own bizarre monastic ceremonies.

One small boy became a sort of fixture, standing like a

graven totem pole, rain or shine, gazing with stony contemplation at the passing expedition members, who were forced
to walk around him as they moved from the cooking fire
to the mess tent. He was about eight years of age, incredibly
dirty, his head partly shaven and his bare feet encased in a
thick protective layer of Beding dirt, which doubtless served
the twofold purpose of keeping him warm in winter and the
numerous midges in a state of frenzied frustration during the
summer. The sleeves of his tattered gray overgarment displayed a modest record of their passages across his continually running nose, leaving rings like the trunk of a severed
tree, accurately cataloguing the passage of time. At this stage
of his development his grubby right hand seemed permanently
fixed to his mouth via the thumb, which, if he ever took out,
must have dazzled him with its unaccustomed cleanliness.

We sat disconsolately in our tents discussing ways and
means of sighting the Snowman, blue bear, Yeti, or whatever
it was and wishing the rain would ease off so that we could
get out and resume the chase, or rather begin it, as we had
hardly had the opportunity to do much. Hillary felt that we
should explore the bush line and eliminate the possibility of
the beast living in or around the rough country below the
present snow line. Once we had satisfied ourselves that it
did not lurk craftily in the thick forest bordering the Rolwaling Valley, we would move on to the higher country
around the Ripimu Glacier and search in the big snow basins,
bordering the line of peaks separating Nepal from Tibet.
While we waited and the rain beat steadily on the plastic
covering over the mess tent, our Sherpa comrades regaled us
with tales and descriptions of their homeland and the various
expeditions in which they had taken part.

I often tried to find out as much as I could about the
Yeti from different Sherpas, hearing a surprising variety of
plausible stories and what could only be described as products
of a fanciful imagination. Much of the information I gleaned
came from Desmond Doig, who could converse fluently with

both Nepalis and Sherpas and who spent much of his time taking note of Yeti lore and trying to clear up stories he had heard about Yeti sightings. I sometimes noticed that, if one pressed hard enough on a particular point of Yeti mythology, the Sherpa questioned would, in an excess of enthusiasm and an earnest desire to please, expound at length on the meeting between a holy lama his grandfather once knew and an enraged Yeti, the unfortunate encounter usually resulting in the escape of a temporarily psychotic lama amid a barrage of stones hurled by the angry Snowman, denied an ecclesiastical supper. These stories were invariably recounted with a mass of pantomime and gesticulation plus a depth and retentiveness of memory equaled only by the elephant.

Even the Nepalis are not averse to a cheering Yeti story, and one lesser government official in Katmandu, who had carried me along on a wave of rhetoric and grandiloquent English, suddenly lost my sympathetic interest when he tried to convince me that the Yeti laid eggs.

At the first sign of an improvement in the weather we were out: one party to set up a Yeti-watching camp on a small plateau at 15,000 feet, the other to install the cameras and telescopes. The first party pitched their tents near a deserted yakherd's hut where they commanded a good view of the rocky slopes opposite, providing there was no mist, and where the Sherpas slept most of the day on the shingled roof of the hut enjoying the warm sun. We of the second party, setting out at Hillary's behest to install the trip cameras, started as a fairly strong team composed of a motley group of Sherpas; Rana, our Nepali liaison officer; Marlin Perkins, John Dienhart, Ed Hillary, and myself. However, because of the unaccustomed altitude, we shed people like an autumn oak shedding its leaves and on arrival at the selected cave a count of heads found three Sherpas, Hillary, and me, with Marlin just in sight, a thousand feet or so below, making his laborious but stately way up the mountainside surrounded by

Sherpas and looking for all the world like John the Baptist among the faithful.

Marlin traveled everywhere at his own steady pace and never failed to reach his objective no matter how far behind the others he fell. He was much older than the rest of us, tall and spare, with a gray beard and well-brushed gray hair, looking far too distinguished to associate with the pack of ruffians fate had forced upon him. Popular with everyone, he excited our admiration by the way he crossed the difficult Tesi Lapcha Pass later in the expedition.

The day began to get very cold, with banks of mist drifting over the passes and sweeping down the valley. It was too chilly to sit around, and as soon as Marlin and his entourage arrived we installed three cameras in the most suitable cave, placing so many cotton trip wires around the entrance and toward the rear that even if we did not photograph anything foolish enough to walk in, we were practically certain to strangle it to death. In fact, it was evident that no large biped frequented the cave, but Marlin Perkins and Hillary were more interested in the photographic record of the smaller animals, such as the pikas and voles, living in the area. With this in mind the trip wires were set only a few inches above the rocky cave floor.

Two days later George Lowe and I moved on to the village of Na, about three hours' walk through stunted forests and over steep muddy tracks, the patches of beautiful autumnal undergrowth giving way to a disorderly array of huge boulders clustered about the stone village. On a grassy bank above the river we pitched our tent, while the remainder of the expedition moved in little groups to turn the campsite into a miniature canvas village.

While we were camped at Na, a small French expedition arrived and established itself about a half mile away from us near the village. Few of us spoke French, but they conversed easily in English and we were able to talk over their proposals for climbing Chobutse, 21,870 feet, a gigantic peak near the convergence of the Tolam Bau and Ripimu glaciers. It looked difficult, seen from the Ripimu, and most of the time we were in the area avalanches could be heard thundering down the precipitous western slopes.

The French unfortunately had a sick Sherpa, Ang Namgyal, about whom they were very concerned and who was convinced that he was going to die. Poor Ang Namgyal had a badly swollen left knee, with swelling and pain in most of his other joints. Tom Nevison diagnosed rheumatic fever. As we had both doctors and medical supplies, Hillary agreed to take care of him in our camp, where he was installed in a private two-man tent only a few yards from our own Sherpas' quarters. Mike Gill (now recovered from his unpleasant bout of pneumonia) and Tom Nevison were able to make him fairly comfortable, but he remained adamant that he was at death's door, as indeed most of us thought he might. As he was a Buddhist, we had expected a studied nonchalance, but, contrary to our rather vague ideas of Buddhist philosophy, he viewed his possible demise with alarm, not to say dismay. His consternation was loud and vociferous, revolving around evil spirits and the need for an all-powerful lama, versed in the necessary incantations and invocations, to exorcise the reluctant demon.

The local lama, well aware that he was on safe ground, now advanced from the village *gompa*, or temple, throwing rice to right and left and muttering prayers as he came. On the one hand, should the unhappy Sherpa die, then the sahibs could be blamed for interfering in the first place; whereas on the other, should he survive, then all power to the great Buddha and extra rice for his devoted servant the humble lama. As George Lowe remarked, whatever the outcome he was "home and hosed."

The sick Sherpa was brought to the entrance of his tent and placed on a couple of sleeping bags, where he could see the mountains and where, incidentally, the sahibs with their cameras would be able to see the ceremony. The lama, it seemed, was not unconscious of the value of publicity. A disgruntled mountain sheep was produced and, after being liberally sprinkled with red ocher, was tied to a stake next to the tent. The lama, still spraying rice about in all directions, squatted alongside the now thoroughly contented Sherpa and began a series of incantations, all the while looking balefully at the resplendent sheep.

After a protracted period of chanting and a visible brightening on the part of the Sherpa the lama suddenly jumped to his feet, spat on Ang Namgyal's knee, rang his bell, and then poured the remainder of the ocher and rice upon the unhappy sheep, with demoralizing effect. The sheep, released from the stake, leaped a nearby stone fence like a startled kangaroo, a sure sign that it was indeed possessed of the indignant spirit. This ended the performance and the lama returned to his village wearing a sportive smile.

Everyone retired, the sahibs perhaps a trifle skeptical, the Sherpas confident, satisfied that all that could be done was done, the rest being up to the gods. This left the sick Sherpa with little option, for he had to do something and do it without delay. Some months later I met him in Solu Khumbu, where he outlined his recovery in a complicated mixture of Hindi and Nepali, punctuated with bursts of laughter and cries of delight. I could not understand the language, but the message was clear enough: sahibs' medicine was fine for headaches and the like, but for anything more serious give him a lama every time.

Obviously belief in the value and efficacy of the lama's ceremony was deeply rooted. This is not unreasonable when one considers our Western doctor-patient relationship; indeed it would almost seem a necessity in similar cases for both patient and physician to stem from similar social and cultural backgrounds.

As the weather cleared in early October, we moved our camp up to higher ground near a lake—the Dudh Pokhari, which is a mile long and rarely freezes over. Our new camp by the Milk Lake, at 16,000 feet, put us in a strong position to cover the large snow valleys of the Ripimu Glacier near the Tibetan border, now less than two miles away. Once again an observation tent complete with telescopes and field glasses was placed on a high lonely ridge, commanding a panorama of peaks and snow fields, the ideal route for Yeti moving over the 19,000-foot passes to the more hospitable Nepali valleys.

No sooner had we made ourselves comfortable at the lake camp than two Sherpas who had been moving loads up to one of the higher camps arrived breathless and wildly excited.

"*Yeti, sahib, Yeti!*" they shouted as they leaped from boulder to boulder down the steep moraine wall behind our tents.

We lost no time, making tracks of our own, straight over the scree and patches of old snow toward the gently sloping snow basin where the Yeti tracks could still be seen, an imperfect line of large prints heading for our camp not three-quarters of a mile away. I was gravely suspicious of these tracks and noted that they followed the same route taken by Hillary, Lowe, Barcham, and me a couple of days previously, when we were returning from a short reconnaissance. Desmond Doig shook my testimony somewhat when he pointed out that "our heavy rubber-soled climbing boots could by no stretch of the imagination sprout toes, heavily balled insteps and smooth elongated heels." I was unconvinced, however, as we had already noted what strange things the sun could do to any prints in the snow, distorting them into all manner of strange shapes and sizes, every one recognizable to the Sherpas as Yeti tracks.

In fact, the Sherpas were generally enthusiastic and more often than not hopelessly inaccurate about the origin of any track they saw, their interpretation having no bearing on the animal being followed, sometimes causing them to follow the tracks backward. As any deer stalker knows, this unorthodox procedure severely limits the probability of the hunter ever catching up with his quarry.

We spent some time with sketch pads, plaster of Paris, and cameras, taking impressions of the prints wherever they were well formed. Finally Hillary called it a day, considering the tracks to be too imperfect to be of any scientific value.

Higher and higher we moved up the glacier, spreading out in small groups in an endeavor to cover as much ground as possible.

Some now felt the effects of altitude and had to ease up a bit until their acclimatization balanced their eagerness and they were able to enjoy moving about the higher country once more. Pat Barcham and Mike Gill, who were both going well, took three Sherpas along the Tibetan border, discovering a parallel pair of Yeti tracks on a ridge between the Menlung and the Ripimu glaciers, at well over 19,000 feet. Hillary, Lowe, Nevison, and I also crossed the border into the Menlung, hoping to see signs near the spot on the glacier where Eric Shipton took his now famous photograph of Yeti tracks. As far as we knew, the Chinese had no mountain troops in the Menlung area, but just in case we took care to keep high. Even so, there was always the possibility of air patrols. We were not anxious to remain long in Tibet proper.

The snow on the other side of the unnamed pass we used proved much too deep for safe travel, so we were reluctantly forced to return, very tired after our unaccustomed exertions above 19,000 feet.

We camped near the pass the next day, made our way down the glacier toward the advance base camp. We were but half an hour from camp when we saw evidence of excitement. Larry Swan had been doing a little exploring above the glacier, when he rounded a hummock and ran straight into a long line of perfect Yeti prints going straight over the ridge and down the valley. We arrived shortly after the discovery, to find the pug marks so clear and crisp that I must confess the hair on the back of my neck stood out like a hedgehog's bristles. I at last faced the immediate possibility of a meeting with the Snowman.

The tracks were, of course, no surprise to the Sherpas, who without hesitation identified them at once as genuine. This time they certainly fulfilled all the required specifications and looked so fresh that I momentarily expected the beast to appear on the glacier below, to which the tracks headed.

They were large and ovoid, broad with toes, and the characteristic spur at the heel clearly shown. I was delighted, for we were within an ace, it seemed, of proving the existence of the enigmatic Snowman, whom I had always wanted to believe in but who had remained just a little too elusive for reality.

As we examined the tracks it grew dark, giving George Lowe just enough time to take a few movie shots before we all returned to camp, anxious to be off the treacherous glacier and back in our tents while we were still able to see. We had no chance of seeing the beast in the dark, and as the tracks ran out over long patches of stony scree farther down the glacier, even less chance of following it to wherever it might be going.

Early next morning the enthusiasts gathered around the prints, photographing, measuring, and taking casts, when Desmond made a startling discovery. He and Marlin, following the tracks down a moderate incline, found that, as they got into firmer snow where the sun barely penetrated, the marks abruptly turned into snow-wolf spoor.

The wolf had come along a short rocky valley, climbed up to the ridge where Larry had made his discovery, and with the connivance of the sun traveled down the same ridge as the Yeti, leaving a clear line of well-spaced giant footprints, turning back into a quadruped as it slipped over the incline out of the glare of the incremental sun. Wherever the trail ran exposed to the sunlight the snow had melted, forming a single large print where formerly there had been two small ones, the spur at the heel caused by the sun shining obliquely down the line of pug marks.

We were disappointed at the diminution of our Yeti. Some were inclined to be skeptical of Desmond's and Marlin's obvious theory. The evidence, however, was clear and was substantially reinforced later when further tracks, pronounced as Yeti's by the Sherpas, disclosed precisely the same change, as they swung over the crest of a shadowed ridge, Yeti on one side and, as Burns put it, "Wee, sleekit, cowrin', tim'rous beastie" on the other.

Several artificial trail-making experiments were tried, leaving the weight of evidence even more heavily against the unfortunate Snowman and convincing the expedition that this was the true explanation for the fabled tracks.

It proved, of course, that a wolf or small animal under certain conditions can leave a trail simulating large biped-like marks, but I saw no reason why it should preclude a Yeti from making Yeti tracks.

Regardless of our investigations the Sherpas harbored no doubts as to the existence of the beast, regarding our observations with amused tolerance and not in the least surprised that we had not actually sighted a Snowman. As Urkein remarked: "How can the sahibs expect to see a Yeti when they parade around the countryside like a herd of lumbering multicolored yaks?"

FOUR

Across the High Pass

Unless you are a mountaineer, an engineer, or a surveyor,
the odds are that the great illumination will escape you, all
your life; You may return to the grave without having ever
known what it is like when the contour lines begin to sing
together, like the Biblical stars.

C. E. Montague

IN A WAY we were not sorry to begin thinking about with-
drawing from the Rolwaling and making the high pass crossing over the Tesi Lapcha into the Everest region of the Solu
Khumbu.

We had enjoyed our excursions in the Ripimu and our
short sojourn in Tibet, but reports by radio from Norman
Hardie indicated the need for more supplies and Sherpa man-
power. He was now ready to erect the Silver Hut, the winter
quarters that Hillary hoped to place as high as possible in the
upper Mingbo Valley.

Hardie and his party, with more than three hundred
coolies, had faced a longer and more arduous journey than
our comparatively low-level walk into the Rolwaling. He
had run into bad weather near a 15,000-foot pass above the
village of Junbesi and been forced to pay off a large number
of his less enthusiastic coolies, while at the same time canvass-
ing the local labor lords for replacements.

The lack of ardor on the part of even the most impervious
of Norm's coolies was understandable. They were well aware
that the 1952 Swiss Everest expedition had lost two men on
the pass under just these same conditions. With continuing

unpleasant weather and much shepherding of porters, the party at last gratefully arrived at Thyangboche Monastery, to be met by the end of the monsoon and a violent local downpour.

At Thyangboche they established radio contact with our Rolwaling party, referring with some justification to themselves as the workers and to us as Hillary's playboys.

Their principal task was to build a hut, largely out of local materials, at about 17,000 feet in the Mingbo Valley. At the same time they were to place all the prefabricated parts for the winter hut on a suitable site around 20,000 feet, in readiness for assembly when the parties joined forces in November.

They had completed most of this program by the time we were ready to cross over and begin the erection of the Silver Hut.

Hillary considered himself more than fortunate in having persuaded Hardie to take the leadership of the Thyangboche party. Norman was recently established in business in Christchurch, New Zealand and was therefore pressed for time. In addition it was his intention to pay a short visit to Japan as soon as we had completed erection of the Silver Hut. Although he was ably assisted by Romanes, Milledge, and Barry Bishop, from the National Geographic Society, Hardie was the only one in the Thyangboche party who had been in the Himalayas before and, unlike the others, could converse fluently with both Sherpas and coolies. He had gained no little fame as a member of the summit party on Kanchenjunga, and both he and his wife had lived for months among the Sherpas of Khumjung. He subsequently wrote a very well-received book concerning the people of the Solu Khumbu.

At this critical stage, when the Thyangboche team was struggling with deep snow near the upper reaches of the Mingbo Valley, our radios were in continuous use, keeping the scattered members of the expedition informed of each other's progress. Although the whole operation was going almost according to plan, all was not well with our communications, we soon found out, once we got close to the Tibetan border.

We used a variety of radio equipment throughout the expedition, including a rather powerful transmitter enabling us to keep in touch with some American amateur radio friends in Katmandu. For local use and the assault on Makalu we had six transistorized New Zealand-built low-power transceivers, and for weather information and news we used battery portable receivers. It was on one of these that we heard Peking radio accuse us of using the Yeti as an excuse to conduct spying excursions along the Tibetan border.

In general we had excellent results from the radio equipment and were able to maintain communications with our field parties over ranges up to twenty-five or thirty miles. For clear interference-free communication a great deal depended on the time of day or night and how deep we had penetrated into the wooded valleys. In any case, as most of our transmissions were from relatively elevated positions we seldom had difficulty in getting a message through. In these early days, however, while the expedition was split in two, with our party in the Rolwaling under Ed Hillary and the other near Thyangboche under Norm Hardie, we were subject to a peculiar and irritating form of interference.

It was our practice to send daily progress reports from each group, so that Hillary could keep his finger on the whole expedition. During one of these talking marathons, as some of them became, the Red Chinese got to us.

Barry Bishop was a peanut fiend, and at one point we were listening to an anguished cry of rage from him, claiming that the Rolwaling party had cornered the expedition supply of salted peanuts, thus reducing the Thyangboche party to a diet of boiled potatoes and tinned peaches. Suddenly his voice was (fortunately, as someone later said) interrupted by the most horrible wailing sound, like a demented dog catching sight of the full moon. We were thunderstruck, to say the least, and were quickly developing a new respect for the range and dissonance of Barry's vocal cords, when Ang Temba excitedly started capering about shouting, "Chinee, Chinee, Chinee wallah."

And so it was. The Chinese, apparently appreciating the importance of the whereabouts of tinned nuts to the "Hillary international spying expedition," decided to deny us that tactical information. From then on, they jammed all our broadcasts while we were in the Rolwaling region.

As we could not alter the frequency of our transmitting equipment and since our newly acquired friends enthusiastically played Chinese operatic records whenever they heard us talking over the air, we resorted to low cunning and switched on suddenly at odd times during the day.

At first this diabolical move threw them off their guard and we were able to get a few messages through, but before long the Chinese *Lohengrin* prevailed and Hillary's voice was lost amid a cacophonous mixture of cries and clashing cymbals.

The radio schedules became a sort of gathering of the clans for the Sherpas. They would arrive from various parts of the camp and collect around the radio set waiting hopefully for the "Chinee wallahs" to begin their regular jamming.

Invariably the performance delighted the gathering, who on one occasion broke into an impromptu dance. Urkein, I learned, had been in Tingri, a village over the border about eight miles away in Tibet, where we suspected the jamming originated. He told me that he had seen radio aerials and several new buildings.

We recognized that we were probably under observation by the Chinese authorities, as indeed we were by the Nepali Government. That we should be thought to be spying on the

Chinese seemed to us ludicrous in the extreme, especially as we could not make a move for miles around without the local people knowing of it.

We began moving our remaining stores back down the Ripimu to the bottom of the Tolam Bau Glacier. From there we hoped to lift our complete camp up to the foot of the icefall in one day.

A big lift and a hard, long day, but the people from Beding, who were to carry most of the loads, took it as a matter of course, being glad of the extra money.

Larry Swan left us at the completion of the Rolwaling Yeti search with the unenviable task of walking all the way back to Katmandu. There he was to collect more fuel and stores, then follow Hardie's route back into the Mingbo, escorting a fresh batch of porters. This suited Larry very well. Traveling at the slow pace of the porters, he would be able to add to his extensive insect collection, while continuing his general biological investigations.

Considering that he left Katmandu in the first place well out of condition and invariably at the rear of the pack, Larry ended up by completely surpassing himself. Quite carried away by his fast-diminishing waistline, he finally took the long high route out to India via Darjeeling, achieving the distinction of having walked farther than anyone else on the expedition.

We also lost John Dienhart, the irrepressible American public relations officer for the World Book Encyclopedia. John was noted for the even tenor of his progression through the Himalayan foothills and became even more notorious for the large bag his Sherpa carried. This contained spare toothbrushes, combs, soap, flea powder, and other toilet necessities Dienhart considered vital for the hundred-mile march into the Rolwaling.

Shortly after our arrival at Beding and after a week of solid rain the "magic of the high Himal" evaporated, as far as John was concerned. He left for the intermittent and somewhat dubious bright lights of Katmandu.

About this time a number of important expedition items had got themselves stuck fast in the hands of the Calcutta customs. Anyone who has been to India will know that this means weeks of inaction, with the probability of certain financial arrangements, invariably to the advantage of the customs officials. However, they little knew the strength of our arm, as John was now fit and ready for battle.

In fact, so keen was he to untangle our customs problems that he set a local record for speed, Beding to Katmandu. We who had been subjected to his high-powered American approach felt an almost fraternal sympathy for the unsuspecting Indian Customs.

Dienhart's going sparked a minor crisis. One of his porters, having drunk too long and too deep of the draught that cheers, gave up all thoughts of load carrying and dumped his forlorn burden, which contained Dienhart's tent, in the middle of the muddy track outside Beding Monastery. Swaying unsteadily, he repaired within, determined to talk the monks into continuing the party begun the night before.

Hillary sent Urkein, our sirdar, after the recalcitrant porter, hoping to persuade him to get going and catch the others before nightfall.

Urkein's disastrous method of persuasion was to crack the porter unceremoniously over the head with a large stick. This would have killed anyone but a hardheaded Sherpa. In this case, however, Urkein succeeded in contributing further to the porter's already stunned condition, leaving him practically immobile for about two days. We kept him in our camp, where Nevison could attend to his wound and where he became known as Splitso.

Repairing Splitso was no great problem, but handling the wrath of the local populace took the hand of a master diplomat. The monks argued that the expedition had added insult to injury by not only splitting the skull of one of their number, but worse, allowing the blood to spill over the *gompa* steps.

Our inexcusable conduct, we found, had placed us in a very bad light with the headman. It took a deal of talking, coupled with the offering of contributions to the *gompa*, before the *status quo* was resumed and peace once more reigned in the Rolwaling.

Unfortunately Dienhart had gone two hours down the trail in heavy rain, unaware that his tent and cooking pots were destined to remain parked outside the monastery for days. However, we were able to get the tent to John before darkness forced him to bed down on the open track.

We began the move toward the Tesi Lapcha in crisp, clear, almost cloudless weather. The sun reflected an intense heat from the sprawling jumble of rocks, dirty ice, and huge boulders making up the terminal moraine of the Tolam Bau Glacier.

In the Himalayas glacial travel is slow, enervating work, the continual clambering up and down sliding shingle escarpments being tiring, apart from deadly dull. Their exertions, coupled with the heat, brought beads of sweat to the foreheads of the warmly clad, laboring Sherpas. Some gave short staccato whistles as they slowly topped the steeper crests. These sounds, they claimed, kept up their strength, but how, I never found out, although I often heard them doing it when the going got heavy. Quite unable to muster a whistle on the steep bits, I was never able to try it for myself. Down the other side in shadows, and out of the direct sunlight, the sweat froze in grimy streaks on their faces, giving them peculiar surprised expressions.

So cold was it in the places where the sun never penetrated that minute flying insects, humming happily through the warm air, were seen to fall lifeless as they passed into the refrigerated depths of the extinguishing shadows.

Pat Barcham and Tom Nevison crossed the pass a few days ahead of the main party, intending to do some exploring and climbing around the peaks near the Everest massive. George Lowe and Marlin Perkins set up a photographic camp on an exposed shelf that stood above the vast stone couloir and gave access to the pass from the Tolam Bau. They expected the two hundred or more fully laden porters to provide a spectacular movie film negotiating the difficult and dangerous stone chute.

The remainder of us were fully occupied sorting and checking loads, while the Beding Sherpas moved the last of our equipment up to the cold stony campsite below the couloir. Here we expected to meet a new batch of Sherpas from Solu Khumbu, who we thought would probably give fresh impetus to the lift over the pass.

On the last day of the move up the Tolam Bau, Hillary and I found ourselves well down the glacier, dispatching the remaining few Sherpas and sorting the final loads. Our dismay knew no bounds when we found all the Sherpas gone, having left two large and unfortunately vital loads still to be taken.

We had obviously gone astray somewhere in our calculations. With only ourselves to blame, nothing now remained but to carry the loads plus our personal gear.

Hillary, taking much the greater proportion of the mountainous pile, staggered off in the wake of several slower-moving Sherpanis. The Sherpa women carried more than forty pounds and seemed hardly to notice the weight as they laughed and chattered with one of their number, a young girl with a three-month-old baby. The mite was warmly wrapped in a woolen shawl and firmly tucked into a cradle that dipped and swayed alarmingly on top of her load.

I brought up the rear, keeping the stragglers moving and whenever possible attempting to hurry them over the most exposed parts of the track.

Much of the route was menaced by high overhanging rock cliffs that fell in parts to a depth of thousands of feet, cut by the Tolam Bau Glacier as it ground its way slowly toward the Rolwaling Valley.

With the barely perceptible glacial movement bringing the cliffs under constant tension we needed to keep moving, at the same time taking care. The long string of Sherpas had no option but to pass under the cliffs, well within range of almost continuous stone avalanches. Every now and again a huge house-sized boulder, loosened from its temporary hold on the edge of the cliff, would come careering down the slopes, bounding into the air and splitting into a hundred pieces. The fragments would crash onto the rocks below and frequently spray the exposed track with a fusillade as deadly as any shrapnel burst.

We made good time, negotiating the worst part of the route without incident, gradually rising higher and higher. We wound our way among piles of fallen boulders and over giant slabs of dirty green ice as the van slowly approached the campsite, immediately below the icefall.

To my surprise, Hillary kept up with the main body, his sweating face screwed in determination as he labored along the broken rocky track. Occasionally he paused at a convenient place, resting his load while he mopped his brow with a small sweat-stained hand towel.

I was long past surprise at any further example of Hillary's unusual powers of endurance, as more than once I had seen him reach a peak of sustained physical activity that few men could hope to equal. In this case he carried more than eighty pounds for six hours at an altitude rising above 17,000 feet, an effort no mountaineer of my acquaintance would care to emulate.

The camp consisted of several tents perched on the top of the moraine wall some hundreds of feet above the glacier. The Sherpas had cleared away the worst of the stones and each tent nestled behind a large boulder, giving a measure of protection from the bitterly cold wind. We were not troubled by the hard stone floors; everyone slept on an air mattress, including the expedition Sherpas, who relished the softer living as much as we did.

Ed and I lay back in our two-man tent, cramped but warm and very tired after an exceptionally hard day.

We drank several cups of hot tea while I got the radio going and spoke to George Lowe, camped a quarter of a mile almost directly above us near the approach to the pass. I went outside the tent. We were now in deep shadow, with the temperature dropping rapidly. A chill wind was sweeping down the glacier from nearby Tibet.

I could see the bulge away up near the top of the cliff, where I knew George and Marlin were camped, but I could see no sign of them. I imagined they were well tucked into their sleeping bags by now. At first sight, it was difficult to see how they could ever have got up the cliff at all. It looked almost sheer, and climbable only with the aid of ropes. A closer inspection, however, showed here and there the vestiges of a track, worming its way upward to disappear around the edge of a rock buttress a hundred feet below the place where I thought George's camp would be.

I felt some apprehension about the coming climb and moved back toward the edge of the moraine wall overlooking the glacier. I now had a better view and the route came into clearer perspective, looking a little more promising than from the bottom of the cliffs. From here I could also see the icefall stretching right across the snow-filled valley, mass upon mass of tumbled ice, completely blocking the way and making the route over the cliffs by far the lesser of the two evils.

I was about to turn back for the warmth of the tent, when, to our mutual surprise, a large black and white lammergeir flew around the edge of a huge boulder not twenty feet from where I stood. The lammergeir, often called the bearded vulture, is not uncommon in the Himalayas, and the expedition saw several, although never as close as this one. It is one of the largest of the vulture family, and I estimated the wingspan of this one to be about ten or eleven feet. He gave me such a calculating look that I involuntarily took a firmer grip

on my ice ax, not relishing the thought of being stuffed
down the throats of his unprotesting children. They, I had
no doubt, were equipped with beaks as fearsome as his and
probably would not split hairs over the odd ice ax or climbing boot attached to their supper.

After a second's thought he turned away, obviously regarding me as something less than tasty and of little culinary
interest.

Using the air currents to turn, he kept his great wings out-
stretched like that of a small monoplane, all the while looking at me indignantly as he banked. In this position he
looked slightly ridiculous, with the thin black band of feath-
ers across his eyes reminding me of an embittered highway-
man.

The following day Hillary and I investigated the icefall.
We thought it might be possible to find an alternate route
should the cliff face and couloir prove too difficult for the
heavily laden Sherpas. Earle Riddiford and Ed Hillary had
made the first European crossing of the Tesi Lapcha in 1951
and had come down the icefall, completely by-passing the
rock gully that now gave us so much concern. Hillary regarded the pass as one of the world's most difficult, and it
had certainly not improved since he last saw it. We could
find no way through the ice, nor around it, so how Ed's
party got down in 1951 became as much a mystery to him as
it was to me.

We arrived back in camp fresh, after a few pleasant hours
on the glacier, just in time to see the first of the Sherpas from
Solu Khumbu arriving for the big lift. We watched them
moving down the cliff face, a number narrowly missing being struck by stones dislodged by their comrades above. Before long the air was filled with the sweet scent of burning
juniper as the porters began cooking with the wood collected
above Thami and carried for three days over the pass.

With more than two hundred loads to move, Hillary decided to send Bhanu Bannerjee and me with sixty laden

Sherpas over first. He intended to follow a day later, bringing the remainder.

Bhanu, having been plucked virtually straight from the
plains of India into the Himalayas, was, not unnaturally, more
than apprehensive now that he was confronted with the
actual crossing. An hour before we were due to start he grew
strangely silent, refusing to speak to anyone, even Desmond
Doig's quiet words of Hindustani drawing little response.
The Sherpas had finished their *tsampa* and tea and were busy
sorting the loads. Those not leaving until the following day
offered spurious advice in a bantering, friendly fashion.

Mike Gill and a Sherpa went ahead to put a rope over the
more difficult part of the climb. Dawa Thondup, my personal Sherpa, and I were preparing to move off without
Bhanu, when he appeared from his tent, boots on, ice ax in
his hand, and a big smile on his face. I was puzzled but too
busy to think much about it. Just as we were leaving, Hillary
called me over to his tent, giving me a small bottle of green
pills. "We've already given Bhanu three tranquilizers, but
here's a few more in case he feels a bit faint higher up." The
mystery of Bhanu's sudden revival was solved. He looked so
ready to tackle any difficulty that I considered swallow-
ing the remainder of the pills myself.

We were soon away, Bhanu, Dawa Thondup, and I in the
lead with the sixty Sherpa porters strung out below in a long,
uneven chain.

Once actually on the cliff face it turned out easier than it
looked, and apart from having to watch for falling stones we
found the climb in the crisp morning air most enjoyable.

In less than an hour we were into the deep couloir where
Mike had begun to secure the fixed rope. The couloir itself
is a long split, running from top to bottom of the mountain
almost vertically, with patches of black greasy ice plastered
to the sides.

We were to make our way across using very delicate
hand- and footholds. Small ledges and knobs of rock provided

enough friction holds to get into the hundred-foot cleft, and from there a thin slab of slippery ice led around a narrow ledge, angling across the bulge of the outer wall to firm ground.

The path led across the couloir about halfway below the summit. It looked unpleasant, but in fact we were more concerned with falling rocks than the actual difficulty of the crossing.

With little or no warning a stone the size of a man's head would come whistling down the rock chute above, crashing from wall to wall as it came, rivaling the speed of an express train. For this reason it was much safer to make the crossing in the early morning, when most of the rocks were still firmly frozen to the heights above.

We roped up and began the crossing, moving one at a time, while I kept the rope firmly belayed in case of a slip. George Lowe and Marlin Perkins appeared on the other side, their movie cameras trained directly across the gap toward the first of the laden Sherpas. These were waiting to follow Mike Gill, who had started stringing the rope in short loops over the steepest parts, and all were now ready to cross.

Bhanu and I were soon safely over, picking our way carefully across to George, who was busy photographing Mike, apparently standing on nothing as he fixed the final part of the rope to the sheer rock wall.

We left George and Marlin to their tasks as we moved on toward a steep track that led to a level area near a rockfall where their two-man tent was perched. Dawa Thondup, observing that we were short of some essentials, "borrowed" a cooking pot and some butter from George's tent as we passed.

I learned later that George, discovering the banditry, turned blue and made several comments, most of them biological, about our antecedents.

We followed the ill-defined track around the edge of the

valley wall, heading toward the upper part of the Tolam
Bau. This put us above the icefall, rather like by-passing
difficult rapids on a river. We intended to camp the night on
the glacier and the next day complete the final part of the
crossing. We would then be over the highest part of the pass
at more than 19,000 feet, leaving only an easy walk into the
Thami Valley leading to the Sherpa capital of Namche
Bazar.

Bhanu and I, with Dawa Thondup, arrived on the glacier
in the early afternoon. A stiff wind had sprung up and we
were soon chilled to the bone. The porters began to arrive
in dribs and drabs, but as I expected, the ones with the tents
and tea-brewing equipment did not turn up until almost dark.
It was a lesson well learned. From then on I took care to see
that only the strongest and fastest Sherpas carried the home
comforts.

We were surrounded by magnificent peaks, long snow
plumes streaming from the summits as a bitter wind blew
down the glacier, chilling our fingers and toes and driving us
to the shelter of the tent.

I unpacked the radio intending to call Hillary and give him
a progress report on the usual evening schedule. Faintly I
could hear him talking to George Lowe, but neither of them
could hear me. After several fruitless calls I checked the batteries, only to find them almost dead flat. The *"jungli"*
Sherpa carrying the transmitter had heard from some of his
more sophisticated friends that we kept a Chinese locked up
in the yellow box. Curious and not afraid of the unexpectedly
diminutive Chinese, he had fiddled with the switches, un-
knowingly leaving the set running all day. Quite oblivious of
my fury, he disgustedly pointed at the set muttering, "Chinee
hogia, finish sahib."

The night was one of the coldest I have ever known and
certainly must have been terribly miserable to the Sherpas.
I managed to pack seven into my four-man tent but the other

fifty odd were forced to find what shelter they could outside.

Bhanu and I had some soup, then walked around the camp to see how everyone was getting on. Five primus stoves were going, cooking communal *tsampa* and tea, and the Sherpas were packed around the flame to get any heat they could and at the same time to keep the wind from blowing the cooker out. Once the meal was over they spread a tarpaulin on the ice, using the loads as a windbreak, then they all piled down together, covering themselves with a large blanket of yak hair.

I went back to my overpopulated tent. In comparison with the hardy characters outside we were living in oriental splendor.

They topped this show of basic ruggedness by a prime example of *savoir-faire*, singing vulgar Sherpa songs all night. Any Europeans attempting to spend the night out in such weather, without sleeping bags or warm coverings of any sort, would certainly have suffered severe frostbite. They all came through it and seemed none the worse.

With cooking problems for sixty people the morning brought disorder, but the wind still blew strongly, so no one was keen to sit around for very long.

In a short time everyone was spread across the glacier making for the bottom of the pass. The men tended to move in small groups, depending on which village they came from. Usually the Khumjung Sherpas would be away first, followed by the four men from Khundi, a smaller village closely related to Khumjung. The Namche Bazar Sherpas usually took a positive delight in being as slow as possible in the mornings. Today, however, the cold wind was my ally and everyone began to move off, anxious to warm up as soon as possible.

The slippery ice made the going difficult for 50 per cent of the Sherpas, who only had smooth-soled straw-filled Tibetan boots. Dawa Thondup and I spent a wearying two hours cutting steps in hard ice, giving the unroped porters a reasonably safe path to follow. Soon after midday we reached the highest point, where a cluster of prayer flags stood stiffly in the breeze, pointing toward the Solu Khumbu, now spread out before us. The colored pennants flew from tall lances embedded in a high cairn of stones, the larger flat stones at the base carved with the inevitable *"Om mani padme hum."* The prayer flags were made of a strong daphne paper (produced from a local variety of that flowering shrub) and were covered in hand-printed Buddhist scripts.

According to custom, each Sherpa added a stone to the cairn, shouting his gratitude for the safe crossing with the familiar words *"Cha-so-so."* Dawa Thondup explained that on these high passes the Sherpa people believed poisonous gases caused the lassitude and headache, often the lot of the unacclimatized.

The Sherpas, only too eager to avoid the wind, kept moving, completely ignoring the splendid view. Bhanu and I remained for an hour enthralled at the spectacle before us, photographing everything in sight and reluctant to leave at all. To our left the Tibetan border, flanked by a long line of snow-clad peaks, lay partly hidden by the bulk of Dongiragutao, almost 23,000 feet high. From Everest, less than twenty-five miles away, swept a panorama of serried mountains, stretching across the horizon, blinding in a mantle of fresh snow. The summit pyramid of the fifth-highest mountain, Makalu, just showed behind them, looking almost insignificant in the hazy distance.

The far side of the pass fell away gently at first, but with increasing steepness where patches of glassy green ice shone through the light covering of snow. Dawa Thondup was already chipping large bucket steps as Bhanu and I arrived ready to give a hand. We moved slowly off the ice and passed into a steep stone funnel leading toward the boulder-spattered slope of unstable scree.

The couloir, not unlike the one above the Tolam Bau Glacier, proved shorter and less spectacular once we were down. We had little difficulty, but Hillary's party, descending the following day, was caught in the midst of a dangerous rockslide. Some loads, mainly chocolate, were lost, but fortunately no one was hurt; the principal casualty resembled the "unknown political prisoner," dropped from a considerable height. Only a close and expert inspection showed that it had once been our short-wave receiver.

That evening we camped by a tributary of the Thami Khola. The place was rough and rocky, but a few sticks of wood were found, which satisfied the Sherpas. Groups of four or five squatted around three big stones forming a fireplace. By pumping vigorously with their goatskin bellows they soon had a fire crackling away, and in a few moments a pot of fragrant tea was brewing.

Above 14,000 feet, of course, fuel becomes a problem. In order to conserve kerosene we used sometimes as many as twenty or thirty men carrying wood up to our base camps. Juniper and dwarf rhododendron are fuels most in use in Sherpa houses, and yak dung and juniper burn well together providing bellows are available. Properly dried yak dung used alone gives off a pleasant smell and burns with a steady hot flame.

Usually our Sherpas had matches, but I have several times seen caravan men light their fires with tinderbox and dry moss, the skin bellows producing a good flame.

The sun left us, the last rays climbing rapidly over the wide hanging buttresses of the peaks around the camp. I stood near the tent enjoying the sunset, when a frightening roar filled the valley. An avalanche, starting high on the slopes opposite, swept toward the valley floor, gathering millions of tons of snow and ice as it came.

The camp shook with a sound like thunder and the valley became obscured by fine snow particles, completely filling the air. The tents and Sherpas received a powder covering, and although we were two miles away from the avalanche the air displaced by the falling mass of snow set both tents flapping.

The next morning the Sherpas seemed strangely slow, finding it necessary to rest oftener than usual and complaining of the loads they were carrying. Bhanu soon found the reason; pointing out that they were afraid we would arrive at Thami too early in the day and that I would make them press on to Khumjung, only half a day further on. I issued a general reassurance and said that not only would we spend the night at Thami, but, to celebrate our safe crossing and on behalf of Hillary, Burra Sahib, I would make a contribution to the Thami Gompa treasury. The resultant meteoric change of pace soon caused me to regret my hasty words as I labored mightily after the fast-disappearing Sherpas.

Thami is the collecting place of hundreds of refugees, driven over the nearby Nangpa La pass by the political troubles in Tibet. The village is a large one, with Sherpa-style two-story stone houses built of yak dung and plaster covering all the available flat space above the junction of the Thami Khola and Bhote Kosi rivers. Across the river, on what had once been the village grazing pastures, more than five hundred refugees were camped. The camp sang with activity, as tall sword-carrying tribesmen moved to and fro across the battered cantilever bridge, some driving yaks or goats, others with heavy bags of grain and salt.

From the protruding ridgepoles of the smoke-blackened yak-hair tents hung strings of sun-dried goat meat, while, tethered about the camp, several large Tibetan mastiffs strained at the scent of strangers. In spite of the strong chain holding each dog and the urging of my Sherpas, I gave up ideas of visiting the refugees and retired to my tent, pitched in a nearby potato field.

Now was a good chance to clean up some long overdue mail. This was interpreted as a sign by the thirsting Sherpas, who vanished with commendable speed into the nearest chang shop.

FIVE

The Solu Khumbu: Home of the Sherpa

Not vainly did the early Persian make
His altar the high places, and the peak
Of earth-o'ergazing mountains, and thus take
A fit and unwall'd temple, there to seek
The spirit, in whose honour shrines are weak,
Uprear'd of human hands.

Byron

SINCE WE FIRST came to Nepal, I had heard stories of Chinese atrocities in Tibet and of refugees being driven over the various passes into India, Nepal, and Bhutan. In Calcutta we had seen a few Tibetans wandering about the streets, mostly in small family groups, looking hot and dispirited.

Katmandu teemed with them, both as refugees and as traders, some from as far away as Lhasa itself. The Swiss Red Cross was doing much to aid them, providing shelter where possible and helping to clothe and feed thousands. They also had ambitious plans to fly a light aircraft carrying grain up to the border where most of the Tibetans were congregated, many of them starving. The expedition was able to help with this project—Hillary intended to construct a small landing field above our base camp in the Mingbo Valley.

At Thami the refugees soon sighted our two colored tents pitched on the edge of a bare potato field overlooking the river. In no time we were surrounded by so many that Pasang was forced to encircle the camp with a climbing rope, which we optimistically hoped would give us a little privacy.

I was also concerned (unjustifiably as it turned out) that some equipment might get stolen in the general confusion. I had no intention of losing any of our sixty valuable loads. Apart from the loss to the expedition, I could be sure of Hillary adding to my personal loss of face and possessions with a few pithy remarks. He had a friendly wit and was fond of ribbing me about experiences we had enjoyed together. I once went astray on the Tasman Glacier in New Zealand, and Ed rarely lost an opportunity to remind me of it. As we shook hands and parted below the Tesi Lapcha, for example, he surmised that in all probability there was more than a slim chance that I would miss the Solu Khumbu altogether and walk right on to Lhasa.

I found that almost all the refugees in the Thami Valley were Khambas. Tall and broad-shouldered, their hair plaited in a long single pigtail, they impressed me tremendously. With no sign of servility they strode about the camp in a swaggering, swashbuckling style, each with a turquoise or coral earring dangling from his left ear and a huge broadsword thrust diagonally through the belt. Their tanned faces, high cheekbones, and aquiline noses reminded me of the North American Indians. By Tibetans the Khambas are regarded as robbers, and with good reason, for once outside their own province of Kham their usual intent is banditry. Wild and lawless, the Khambas hated the Chinese invaders and had given them so much trouble that all those the Chinese could neither kill nor capture were driven over the border.

Unfortunately the valleys of the Solu Khumbu could feed only the animals and people of the thinly spread Sherpa population. There was no shortage of space, as the majority of the higher valleys are almost uninhabited, being completely unproductive. A few provide grazing for yaks, but only during the summer months. The refugees, arriving at the rate of two or three a day and usually bringing their animals with them, soon used up what little spare grazing was to be found. The Sherpas recognized the problem, but as they regarded all Tibetans as cousins they could only welcome them and hope they would soon move on to someone else's pasture. As far as I could see, the lamas welcomed the Khambas and encouraged them. Why not? After all the Khambas were strong supporters of the church, invariably giving generously, more often than not of someone else's money. As the monks philosophically pointed out, those robbed doubtless intended to contribute to the *gompa* in any case.

The Nepalese Government, which administered the Solu Khumbu district, hoped gradually to move the Tibetans down toward the lower Nepalese valleys, but this was necessarily a long-term plan. In the meantime the Red Cross people were doing everything possible to bring food into the area, being particularly conscious of the approaching winter.

As far as the animals were concerned the food shortage was obvious. Dead goats, yaks, and sheep lay about along most of the Thami Valley, often right on the track or in the streams. No one bothered to bury the carcasses, just leaving them wherever they happened to fall. Decay and stench permeated the whole valley. One needed a strong stomach and a stout heart a day's walk each side of Thami. Meat was so cheap that I bought a whole sheep for little more than one shilling.

The Khambas gathered about our tents inspecting everything, talking excitedly, and frequently pointing at me. They have their own dialect, but as it is similar to the Sherpa language they were able to speak directly to Dawa Thondup and Pasang.

"Why is the sahib here?"

Dawa Thondup explained that the sahibs with Burra Sahib were here to climb the mountains and were unafraid of the gods. The Khambas were unimpressed with me. Dawa Thondup, quick to seize an opportunity, added inaccurately, "The sahib comes from England and is very powerful."

The Khambas, still stolidly unimpressed, parried with, "How many sons has the sahib?"

"*Chu*" (ten), replied Dawa, throwing all caution to the winds.

This outrageous lie was accepted with obvious satisfaction and vociferous approval. Crossing over to the group, I was at first astonished, then delighted to receive a generous row of stuck-out tongues from the now eagerly admiring Khambas. I might not have received this universal Tibetan sign of respect quite so well had I known that it stemmed from the magnitude of their regard for my prowess rather than sheer personal charm.

Dawa Thondup's secret disapproval of my having no sons came to a head one evening when he questioned me through Bhanu.

"Is it true that Peter Sahib has no sons?"

Bhanu replied that this was indeed a statement of fact.

"Is it possible, then, that Peter Sahib has sons which he chooses not to talk about?" inquired Dawa Thondup hopefully. This pointedly embarrassing remark was denied with some heat after Bhanu, interest quickening, translated.

"Well, then," retorted Dawa Thondup with finality, "tell Peter Sahib he must change his wife." Months later, when my wife visited Nepal and was staying in Dawa Thondup's house, I reminded him of his solution to what he considered a major domestic problem. Looking her straight in the eye with an enviable aplomb, he observed that Peter Sahib must have misunderstood, as he, Dawa Thondup, would certainly never dream of suggesting such an unholy thing.

He maintained a keen interest in my family, often asking quite penetrating questions concerning New Zealand and our way of life. Like all Sherpas, whose lives are bound up with any animals his family may own, he was quite unable to imagine a country with no yaks.

He once said, "Peter Sahib, you must own many yaks in your country." I replied, "No, Dawa Thondup, no yaks." "But, Peter Sahib, your family surely is wealthy and has yaks otherwise you could not own all this costly equipment."

I explained at some length that my family were far from wealthy and were not only devoid of yaks but there were, in fact, no yaks at all in New Zealand. He received this piece of intelligence with astonishment, his face assuming an "I thought so" look as I went on to describe our beef and dairy cattle. With patience, plus a certain Old World charm, he waited until I had finished. Then he remarked simply, "Peter Sahib, those are yaks. It's just that you don't know what to call them."

Confusion increased when Dawa Thondup inquired of Bhanu, "As Peter Sahib has no yaks, how then does he earn his living?"

Not an unreasonable question, but a difficult one to answer to anyone who had never seen a really large lake before, never mind the sea. After an unconvincing attempt at describing my occupation as a naval officer, coupled with Bhanu's fanciful, not to say fictitious, impression of the magnitude of the Pacific Ocean, Dawa Thondup gave up.

"Peter Sahib does not tell the truth, for if this Pacific lake is as big as he claims surely the water would fall off the edge of the world." For the first time I realized that he thought the world was flat. Indeed I found all our Sherpas thought so. Their arguments proved so convincing that I began to have grave doubts myself.

Sherpas generally regard the Europeans as expert in almost everything except the Buddhist religion or the niceties of the Sherpa social customs. Sahibs who could speak Nepali or Hindustani were held in the highest regard, and people like Desmond Doig or Norman Hardie had a special place in the affections of the Sherpas.

The Khambas continued to ask questions about me. I was particularly struck by one fierce-looking fellow who wore baggy trousers and leather-topped boots. A long red tassel hung down from the end of his pigtail, and his arm and part of his chest were exposed, leaving the empty sleeve of his shuba hanging from his shoulder. A sword and dagger were thrust into his waistband, and a tinderbox hung at his hip.

He stood apart, one hand on the hilt of his sword, eying the camp, doubtless estimating the worth of our goods in the Tingri bazaar. To my everlasting disappointment the fierce

robber-chief effect was spoiled by the large pale blue um-
brella he held aloft and by the way he abandoned all pre-
tense at dignity, jumping over a low stone wall in panic when
our pressure cooker blew off steam with a loud roar.

An equally rough-looking man, who departed as unceremoniously as the robber chief, was without his right hand at
the wrist. This, I learned, was punishment for some crime
committed in Tibet.

Tenzing of Everest was born in Thami. We heard that his
mother still lived here, but we never saw her, nor did we
find out which house she lived in, she apparently having become a recluse. As soon as we could Bhanu and I visited the
monastery, here we were told we would see a *rimpoche*, a
reincarnate lama.

The monastery wore a festive air, with gaily colored
prayer flags flying from every vantage point and Sherpas or
Tibetans crowding every inch of space. We had great difficulty in even seeing the *rimpoche*, so dense was the mass of
people. Bhanu discovered that preparations were being made
for the cremation of an important lama from Tibet. He had
died many years ago and been embalmed. He had been ven-
erated until the coming of the Chinese.

The Tibetans knew from painful experience that the Chinese were no respecters of religion, so they smuggled the
body over the Nangpa La to Thami. Now, on the instructions of an oracle, it would be cremated, and a stupa built
over the ashes.

A messenger from the *rimpoche* approached.

Were we the Americans who were to liberate Tibet?

No.

Were we Americans?

No, but Hillary and an American would arrive tomorrow.

Did we have a contribution for the *gompa?*

I paid over some money, and as there seemed to be no
further interest in us we left for camp. I later learned that

Hillary had been questioned closely by the *rimpoche* on the possibility of his going to America.

We were halfway to Khumjung the next day when a sharp-eyed Sherpa pointed to a distant figure rounding a bend in the track. "Hardie Sahib." I was immensely pleased to see Norm and spent an enjoyable hour listening to his unvarnished account of the Thyangboche party's activities. He was anxious to get on, intending to meet Ed near Thami. He traveled alone and, I suspected, pretty fast, so I was quite content to wander along in the opposite direction. We headed toward Khumjung, where Bhanu and I had an invitation to stay the night at Dawa Thondup's house.

The track wound along the valley's edge, gradually climbing higher and higher above the river. We were clearly drawing closer to Khumjung, as evidenced by the quickening pace and the less frequent stops for chang. Overhead, vultures wheeled and circled as they hunted dead animals in the short scrub. They flew heavily, obviously gorged and doubtless delighted at the unexpected feasting provided in the Thami Valley.

There is no gradual approach to the Everest region from the Rolwaling. Apart from the magnificent view at the top of the Tesi Lapcha the mountains are hidden by the hillsides. It is only just before Khumjung, where the track crosses over the hill, that the full majesty of the peaks bursts across the vision. Immediately in the foreground Kangtega and Tamserku rise, serene and inviolable, the summits touched with the first of the afternoon mists. To the left Khumbila, the Sherpa god mountain, stands above the twin villages of Khumjung and Khundi. Ama Dablam, like a giant white bat, appears half crouched across the valley, surely the most spectacular of Himalayan peaks, a wonder to the mountaineer's eye. In the distance at the head of the valley, the five-mile length of the Lhotse-Nuptse wall obscures all but the bare black topmost triangle of Everest. A sure sign of wind,

a long snow plume streams from the summit, partially ob-
scuring Lhotse Shar, the highest unclimbed peak in the world.

We by-passed Namche Bazar, the track leading above this
important Sherpa village, and plunged down past a *mani* wall
toward Dawa Thondup's house. He and Pasang had gone
ahead to prepare for visitors. In a few minutes we were at the
house, followed by a throng of Sherpa children who had
spied us passing through the potato fields. While Dawa
Thondup's wife welcomed us, Bhanu kept the children at
bay by telling them that the sahib had a baby Yeti imprisoned
in his rucksack. They professed to disbelieve this, but I
noticed that none were anxious to come too close to my
pack. In the manner of penguins standing at the ice edge
they tried to propel the smallest and grubbiest child alongside the rucksack first, on the principle that a small sacrifice
might be in order if it ensured the safety of the majority.

Dawa Thondup's wife was not tall, but she was well pro-
portioned and graceful, with prominent cheekbones and al-
mond eyes. Her jet-black hair hung in two plaits down her
back; into each plait red wool had been interwoven and the
ends formed into large tassels reaching to her waist.

The dangling sleeves of her robe were turned back at the
wrists, showing the bright blue silk lining. She wore two
striped woolen aprons, indicating womanhood, one at the
front, the other at the back, while around her neck hung several huge blood-red coral beads spaced with the pearls of
Tibet, the *zi*. These so-called pearls are oblong-shaped, agate
in color, laced with black veins that have white borders in
a roughly circular shape. The *zi*, the most valued of the
Sherpa's jewelry, are sometimes worth many hundreds of
rupees and are worn by all Sherpas, men, women, and children.

Leaving our packs below, we crossed the dirt ground floor
of the house, climbing the short wooden stairs to the top
floor and living quarters. I sat on a wooden stool by the open
window while my eyes accustomed themselves to the gloom.

The room was clean and spacious but very badly lit, the only light coming from three small windows set along one wall. There were no chimney and no hole to let out smoke. The fire, which was alight, burned on a stone slab near the back wall and the smoke just drifted upward, blackening everything above standing level, eventually drifting out through cracks or junctions in the roof.

At one end of the room, on shelves, were wooden chests of flour and grain. Against the large square central pillar of the house stood a big wooden barrel holding the water supply, while a low sleeping platform was piled with rolled-up bedding at the far end of the room. On top of this unruly pile Dawa Thondup's three-year-old son lay face downward fast asleep. He had waited all day for the arrival of his father and at the last moment had dropped off, missing the excitement of the return of a father loaded with presents. In accordance with Sherpa custom, a bowl of *rakshi* (a potato or rice spirit) was handed to us by the hostess; by custom we refused. I had learned that the Sherpa housewife is trained early in the conventions of entertaining guests. She offers the *rakshi* three times, each time filling the bowl to the brim. The guest politely refuses but invariably allows himself to be persuaded. I could not drink much of the spirit, so I usually kept my glass fairly full by taking small sips, thus leaving little room for overreplenishment. I have on occasion noticed that the true Sherpa *rakshi* enthusiast gets over the niceties as quickly as possible, settling to the more serious drinking as early as decency permits.

Dawa Thondup had a wonderful faith in the efficacy of *rakshi*, not only to rub on wounds but as a stimulant to greater effort on the mountain. He always carried a small bottle about his person, never failing to produce it and press the rather muddy contents upon me when the path became particularly steep. He said the only way to reach the top of any mountain was to drink *rakshi* and never eat butter with boiled potatoes. Butter, he claimed, caused a weakness about the knees and a loss of power.

I regret to say that on Makalu the following year poor Dawa Thondup found himself unable to go above Camp III and was sent down to work in the lower camps. It could hardly have been due to the *rakshi* shortage, as I have never known him to be without a little in his rucksack. He must have inadvertently eaten butter with potatoes.

I was fond of Dawa Thondup and very disappointed that he was unable to go high, but, like several of our Sherpas, he was prone to severe high-altitude headaches and sickness. At lower altitudes his assets were strength and stamina, loyalty and courage. He could also be temperamental and individualistic, as are most Sherpas.

By the time we had eaten a meal of potatoes boiled in their jackets, the remainder of the porters began to arrive. One by one they piled their loads around the tent that Pasang had carefully pitched in a corner of the Thondup courtyard. Bhanu and I decided to spend the night in our own tent, as Dawa's family seemed to be inundated with relatives who managed to take up all the sleeping room in the house.

The morning brought a cold mist, plus about twenty Sherpanis, instead of the expected porters. Many of the porters lived in Khumjung and after the night's celebrations had found themselves unable to rise, so their wives had come in lieu. Fortunately I had not paid them yet or the wives probably would not have turned up either. The Sherpa is not overly concerned with time, and he much prefers to let his wife carry the load if possible. This often gives him a chance to collect a further load and thus double pay or, at the least, extra time to drink chang.

I was not in the least worried about the ability of the Sherpanis to complete the lift, as the women of Khumjung were well noted for their stamina and carrying capacity. It was more a question of collecting them together, getting them going, and then keeping them on the move. Khumjung is a considerable distance from the nearest spring, and the village Sherpanis have long since got used to carrying eighty or ninety pounds of water several times each day to their respective homes. Generations of water carrying and potato digging have given the ladies a disquietingly casual approach to an expedition's comparatively puny loads.

The average Sherpa sees nothing unusual in his pregnant wife carrying a load equal to his own. In fact he prefers that she should, thus leaving him free to attend to the more important matters at hand. The family's yaks must always be seen to and during the climbing season he finds himself fully occupied watching over the countless needs of the invading sahibs.

The Sherpas use but an infinitesimal amount of the enormous power available to them in the swift-flowing mountain rivers. And then only for turning prayer wheels or grinding a small amount of grain. Why worry about water power when they have the cheapest and most readily available source of power in the world—woman power!

Thyangboche is dedicated to the contemplation of the Everest massif. Except perhaps for its brother establishment, Rongbuk, on the Tibetan side of Everest, it would be impossible to find a more desirable site for such contemplation and meditation.

The monastery commands superb views in every direction, the view downward as impressive as the upward one. Below Thyangboche the Dudh Kosi cuts through an enormous gorge, its raging torrent clearly audible from within the rhododendron-shrouded monastery, perched on the edge of the spur hundreds of feet above.

With certain exceptions no women may remain in the vicinity of the monastery after nightfall. I once jokingly expressed my concern about this to Annulu. He thought for a moment, his face creasing into a huge grin. "Peter Sahib not worry," he said. "Plenty Sherpani nunnery just little ways down the track." As one who enjoyed a reputation for charming the ladies, he more than likely knew what he was talking about. Anyway he took delight thereafter in implying that I was concerned for myself rather than for the Thyangboche monks.

After a short rest for lunch of cold boiled potatoes in the monastery courtyard we hurried on to Chanmitang. I was anxious to meet Wally Romanes, Jim Milledge and Barry Bishop, who I knew would be there, while the Sherpas were equally anxious to receive their pay.

That night the whole expedition gathered in Khumjung. Ed Hillary and his Rolwaling party were setting up tents in an empty potato field just as our Thyangboche party arrived from Chanmitang. Dr. Griffith Pugh, in charge of the scientific program, arrived from Katmandu with fifty loads of special equipment.

Griff presented an astonishing sight. Tall and pale, crowned with a crop of blazing red hair, he wore a bright orange down jacket reaching to his knees, and azure-blue padded trousers. This garb, coupled with a white plaster of sunburn cream, gave him the appearance of a myopic lobster. Slow and deliberate, Griff had the amusing ability to end a perfectly ordinary story with an unusual and often risqué twist. He fell from grace shortly after the winter when he collected the mail from Katmandu, stuffed it into his rucksack, and promptly forgot about distributing it for more than a week. On an expedition a crime of this sort ranks as more than heinous and is rarely forgiven.

Griff later redeemed himself by finding a couple of bottles of scotch, also lost with the mail.

We could hardly claim to be starved of letters, as runners left Katmandu at regular intervals, providing us with mail every ten days or so.

The next day we moved on to Chanmitang, sorted two hundred loads of stores, engaged fresh porters and began the long haul up to the Green Hut. Hillary had envisaged the hut as an emergency building, rough but substantial, a safe place to retire to should the winter quarters become untenable or some emergency occur.

Wally Romanes, who had charge of construction, built the hut along the lines of a New Zealand bush hut. Warm and comfortable, it had four bunks, a stove range for heating and cooking, a window, a radio, and a full-size-sahib door. We had all bumped our heads on the low Sherpa entrances, and Wally took pleasure in watching the Sherpas who came into the Green Hut automatically and quite unnecessarily bending double.

Leaving Chanmitang on the morning of April 12, we reckoned on reaching the Green Hut by late afternoon. The route passed through the partially deserted summer village of Pangboche, below the southern face of Ama Dablam. Crossing innumerable snow-filled basins, it wound with increasing steepness toward the bottom of the Mingbo Glacier, where the canvas-covered Green Hut stood amid a pile of moraine boulders and scree.

Anxious to get on and try ourselves at higher altitudes, we advanced in two groups. The lightly laden sahibs took the van, while the Sherpas, wearing an assortment of pained expressions, came on at a speed dependent on the state of their health, after the festivities of the night before.

The pace set was a hot one, a rapidly developing competitive spirit urging the sahibs on, perhaps to the detriment of their peace of mind. Hillary, Nevison, and myself were wearing canvas shoes and soon began to pull away. The others, struggling to keep up, dropped behind one by one as the unaccustomed weight of their boots slowed them down. Used to the more sophisticated European footwear, the Americans viewed our plain New Zealand-made climbing boots with considerable disfavor, even referring to them pungently as "Hillary cowbalers." We had mostly worn canvas shoes for the walk in from Katmandu, some changing to boots at Thyangboche, a few lasting in lighter shoes as far as the Green Hut. From there on above 17,000 feet, of course, boots had to be worn all the time.

It soon became evident that Hillary intended to show Nevison and me a thing or two about high-speed Himalayan travel. For an hour or so all went well and we remained close together, not a word passing between us as we concentrated on an extreme of effort. With the increasing altitude the degrees of acclimatization and fitness quickly became evident as Nevison first, then Hillary, began slowly to pull away. Try as I might, I was unable to keep up and on arrival at the Green Hut found that I was about ten minutes behind Hillary, who had come in second to Nevison. Hillary was clearly rather surprised at this astonishing burst of power displayed by Nevison, who had now, however, run himself into the ground and was unable to get any higher for a couple of days. This was typical of Tom Nevison, who seemed able to produce great reserves of nervous energy when he most needed it, a fortunate accomplishment that was later to stand him in good stead the following year on Makalu.

The next morning we ascended the glacier following the route prepared by Hardie, to find a small snow field immediately below the 19,600-foot Ama Dablam Col. Here we began the erection of the Silver Hut, so named because of its outer skin of aluminum paint. Within three weeks the hut was complete, bunks and kerosene heater installed, heavy batteries carried up, and wind generator operating. I began to envy the scientific party who would obviously have a comfortable and secure haven should the winter weather prove as unpleasant as we had been led to believe. I would have liked to remain for the winter, but Hillary and I were due to return to New Zealand for a few weeks to arrange a second shipload of stores.

As the Silver Hut neared completion, people began to disappear in all directions, some to climb, and some back to Khumjung. Others seemingly just vanished into thin air. I had little doubt that the final task of clambering around the outside of the hut in the cold wind, filling innumerable seams with sticky tape, was responsible for the exodus. Before I could concoct a good excuse and escape for a little private climbing myself, I became a victim of my own tardiness and was landed with the unwelcome task.

In fact, however, I was helped considerably by Barry Bishop, the only one remaining at the hut, who was preparing his glaciological program. I knew that Hillary encouraged any well-planned private climbing trip, and I expected that my intention to go up to the Everest icefall would meet with approval once the hut was completed.

At about this time I received a letter, carried by runner for eight days from Katmandu to Khumjung and by Sherpa the three days up the Mingbo Glacier to the Silver Hut. It read: "The Naval Board hereby appoint you to Her Majesty's New Zealand Ship WAKEFIELD and direct you to repair forthwith to your duty. . . ." I certainly would have had no little difficulty had I really been expected to repair forthwith; however, I probably now hold the honors as the only naval officer ever to receive a letter of appointment at 20,000 feet.

Back at Chanmitang I laid plans for my Everest trip, while Hillary, Desmond Doig, and others prepared to walk out to Katmandu with Khunjo Chumbi, who was an elder of Khumjung, and the Yeti scalp from Khumjung. The scalp, claimed to be genuine, was to be examined by experts and so would have to go to the United States, where, presumably the Snowman experts lived. Khunjo Chumbi came along as guardian of the scalp.

With a keen sense of exhilaration Dawa Thondup, Nima Dorje, Ang Tsering, and I, barely conscious of our heavy packs, dropped down the rhododendron-fringed path to the bridge across the Imja Khola gorge. Taking photographs from a rise above the bridge, I noticed several musk deer striking casually up the river bank past the Sherpas toward the nearby monastery. Like the numerous monal pheasants in the area the deer have come to realize that they are quite safe from harm within the precincts of Buddhist Thyangboche.

For six carefree days we roamed at will around the Everest region, on our third day reaching a point a little under 20,000 feet on unclimbed Pumori. From here we had a clear view into the western cwm and across the Lho La to the North Col in occupied Tibet.

Pleased with our efforts but chilled by a cutting wind, we returned to Lobuje, near the bottom of the Khumbu Glacier, where we spent the night in one of the two stone yak-herders' huts.

Early the following morning we arrived at Phalong Karpo to find the bridge over the Chola Khola washed away. With the air temperature at about plus ten Fahrenheit, wading the near frozen river became an exercise carried out with the alacrity of Fijian fire walkers. All made it, all, that is, with the notable exception of Nima Dorje, the most diminutive of our little band although probably the most celebrated, for he once stood on the summit of Dhaulagiri with the Swiss. Nima had inadvertently submerged when his foot slipped. His heavy load took him peremptorily to the bottom, from where he emerged on the far bank making unintelligible but clearly impolite observations on the backgrounds and ancestry of the other Sherpas, by now almost collapsed with mirth.

Normally we would not have needed to cross the river at this point, but Hillary had asked me to take a look at Taweche, the 21,300-foot unclimbed peak now directly between us and Thyangboche. For two days we camped below the southern face of Taweche beside a wide frozen lake, the surface covered with large slabs of ice that had fallen from the cliffs above and skated for hundreds of yards, giving a peculiar sugar-cake effect to the lake. Nima and I investigated possible routes on the peak, reaching an altitude of about

18,500 feet, all we felt we could safely manage. From above that point the climb looked exceedingly difficult and would doubtless tax to the utmost a much more competent party than ourselves.

By December 3 we had returned to Chanmitang and in company with Bhanu began a journey that ended eight days later in Katmandu. Here, while Bhanu went on to Calcutta, I sorted stores and wandered happily around the city waiting for Hillary's return with Khunjo Chumbi and the Yeti scalp.

The day after we arrived in the Nepali capital city an uprising took place, apparently directed against the King, but nobody seemed to take much notice or to mind very much. The Prime Minister, Mr. Koirala, was dismissed and confined to his office by order of King Mahendra Bikram Shah, a string of minor officials landed in jail, and Gurkha troops rushed about the streets for a few hours. By next day all was quiet. Rumor had it that the King was afraid to come out of his palace because someone might throw a bomb at him. A fairly unlikely possibility, I should have thought, as Katmandu teemed with police and Nepali soldiery.

I waited the return of Khunjo Chumbi with interest, anxious to hear his impressions of the New World. When told that he was to accompany the scalp to the United States, he had prepared for the journey by packing plenty of brick tea and sun-dried meat, as he would upon leaving for Tibet. Desmond Doig managed with some difficulty to dissuade him from these arbitrary arrangements, but could not shake his belief that there is no inhabited place in the world that does not have flies. With this in mind he had prepared two yak-tail fly whisks, with silver handles, to be presented to the headmen of the English and American villages. I do not know how he made out with the American one, but he presented the English one to a somewhat nonplussed Queen's Equerry at Buckingham Palace. Perhaps fortunately for her, the Queen was away at Sandringham at the time, although later, as the guest of King Mahendra in Katmandu, she expressed

the desire to meet Khunjo and Mrs. Chumbi, who were so
charmed by the occasion that they named their newborn son
Philip Tobgay Chumbi in honor of the Duke.

Hillary arrived with the now discredited scalp, which had
unfortunately been adjudged by various experts as very convincing and very old but undoubtedly a fake, as it had apparently been made from the hide of the serow, a Himalayan
goat.

I was to take Khunjo back to Khumjung by helicopter,
a mere two-hour flight compared with the more normal
seventeen-day walk in. As he had flown halfway around the
world, I had expected him to take the helicopter flight in
his stride like any well-traveled Tibetan. Sitting under a
plastic bubble right in the nose of the helicopter must have
unnerved him, for, from the moment we took off, he kept
his eyes tight closed and began a low chant, all the while
fingering his prayer beads. I became so concerned for him
that I pressed the pilot to increase speed that we might sooner
get him back to the ground and among his friends. I needn't
have worried, for the pilot was already making all possible
haste. Not, as I soon found, from a concern for Khunjo's
welfare, but because of the singularly curious and fulsome
stench that began to emanate from Khunjo's person. I had
long been familiar with the aroma sometimes associated with
the more proletarian of the Sherpa community, but I must
confess that this emanation was new to my experience.

The pilot had just remarked that Khunjo could probably
float home the rest of the way without a helicopter, when
I found the cause of the trouble. The strong sun shining
through the clear plastic hood of the cockpit had heated
Khunjo's embroidered felt, knee-high boots beyond endurance and now the uncured leather soles bore witness to their
original source. With what may have seemed unceremonious
haste we dropped down onto a potato field at Khumjung,
thankfully giving up Khunjo to his admiring family and
friends.

The village headmen produced four white muslin cere-
monial scarves, one for each of us plus one for the helicopter. With the imminent possibility of decapitating a couple
of hundred Sherpas we took off, leaving Khunjo already
well away, spreading tantalizing rumors of the home of the
sahibs. Surrounded by the whole village, he held at arm's
length a calendar, each page demonstrating in near nudity
the overpaid symbol of civilized sex, an American film star.

SIX

The Climb Begins

"I hold that a man should strive to the uttermost for his
life's set prize."

> Lines from Browning engraved
> on Shackleton's headstone,
> South Georgia

IN JANUARY 1961, Hillary and I returned to New Zealand
for a few weeks. There we arranged shipment of more supplies to our agents in Calcutta and helped our wives prepare
for the rigors of their own expedition. The so-called Ladies'
Expedition, under the generalship of Lady Hillary, was composed mainly of the wives of some of the Makalu expedition
members. The ladies planned to walk the 180 miles to
Everest, enjoying the scenery, which is at its most picturesque during the months of February and March, then fly
out to Katmandu from our airstrip in the Mingbo Valley.

Fred Moody, a well-known Auckland doctor who had
long wanted to visit the Himalayas, was invited to accompany
the party. Tall and fit-looking, Fred strode happily through
the Himalayan foothills with the lordly dignity of a Harley
Street specialist. He was followed by his apprentice and
personal Sherpa, Annulu, who carried the medical bag and
acted as assistant surgeon. Fred's evening clinic became immensely popular, and as the word soon spread our evening
camps were usually crowded with villagers clamoring for
the doctor sahib's attention.

Presumably as a relic of his wartime associations, Fred
insisted on addressing all Sherpas as George, regardless of
size, shape, or sex. Normally this little idiosyncrasy could

reliably be expected to cause unlimited confusion among our camp followers, but not so with Fred. Guided by some hitherto undiscovered sixth sense, the right Sherpa always seemed to appear in answer to his shouted "George."

One of our Sherpas, a diminutive character named Hakpa Norbu Khundi, appeared at Fred's medical meet late one evening. He had a fiery red carbuncle on his wrist which must have caused him considerable pain, although he never lost his cheery smile. The doctor sahib cleaned the wound and wrapped a piece of sticking plaster around Hakpa's wrist. Louise Hillary delighted Hakpa by drawing a wrist watch on the sticking plaster with her fountain pen. For a few days Hakpa proudly paraded around the camp with his sleeve rolled up, so that none would miss the sahib type watch. One day I noticed the plaster missing and asked him about it. "Oh, Peter Sahib," he said with a grin, "I sold the watch to a passing Tibetan." Con men, it seems are not entirely confined to the Western world.

By February 1961 we were back in Katmandu with a large assortment of supplies for restocking the storehouse at Chanmitang and for the assault on Makalu. Two more mountaineers joined us at the Hotel Royal, Leigh Ortenberger, from California, and John Harrison, from New Zealand. Both men were well-known climbers, Ortenberger having had extensive experience in the Andes and Harrison a fine record both in the New Zealand Alps and the Himalayas. These additions were part of Hillary's policy to bring in new and vigorous blood in case the long period of altitude was taking its toll on the winter party.

On March 2 we gathered at the village of Banepa with almost two hundred Nepali porters and fifteen or so of our permanent Sherpas. This was the season of flowers. The hills were ablaze with crimson rhododendrons. About our campsites deep purple primulas nestled on ledges and crannies of the rocks, and beside the streams and in the fields were banks of purple asters, glades of creamy peonies, and tall, elusively perfumed daphne. Giant magnolias were coming into bloom, and delicately petaled orchids flowered among the moss-trimmed trunks of every shady tree.

Over great mountain ridges and across tumbling alpine streams we went. The days slipped by, with walking in the early morning and resting or sleeping during the heat of the day. There was no hurry and we were content to match the steady ten miles a day maintained by the porters.

On March 20 we reached our 15,000-foot Mingbo base camp, where we reunited with the winter party. They had had a very successful winter, with only two stormy periods confining them to the Silver Hut.

In addition to their exceptionally productive scientific program they capped the winter with a magnificent first ascent of Ama Dablam, the spectacular 22,494-foot peak almost at the front door of the Silver Hut. Over three weeks of very high-standard climbing put four men on the summit, an Englishman, an American, and two New Zealanders. This unquestionably very difficult climb, was led by Michael Ward, a surgeon of London Hospital, England, who, with Dr. John West of the British Medical Research Council, Dr. S. Lahiri of Calcutta University, and Captain S. Motwani of the Indian Army Medical Corps, had joined Griffith Pugh to winter in the Silver Hut.

By arrangement with the International Red Cross, which owned a Pilatus Porter—an outstanding high-altitude-performance aircraft, Hillary agreed to construct a five-hundred-yard airstrip in the Mingbo. The Red Cross wanted to fly in food for the Tibetan refugees and we needed some assistance with air transport, so we were able to co-operate usefully. The strip was constructed by hand, using Sherpas and some Tibetans who were paid by the expedition. During much of the winter they worked, chopping off frozen clumps of snow grass, filling in holes and rolling away large boulders. Near the take-off end of the strip were two huge boulders weighing all of twenty tons each. We were unable to break them up, nor could we roll them, as they were partly buried and much too awkwardly shaped.

We racked our brains for a solution to the problem and in the end decided to send to Katmandu for explosives. When the Sherpas heard of our dilemma they approached Hillary. "The problem is a simple one, Burra Sahib," they said. Mindful of something about not seeing the wood for the trees, we watched them at work. They dug an enormous crater beside each boulder, then simply levered them into the holes and buried them.

It was now March 22 and time for my wife June and Louise Hillary to return to New Zealand. The Pilatus Porter was parked at the top end of the sloping airstrip with large rocks under each wheel. They climbed in while Dawa Thondup and I ran to the take-off point to wave farewell. The motor was given full power and the plane shook as the rocks were suddenly removed. Like a drunken duck the aircraft ran uncertainly along the rough surface, gathering speed and swaying, as the wheels struck hidden holes. I felt physically sick as the pilot, at the last minute, pulled back the stick, banked to miss a small hill, and flung the plane into space over a steep precipice, right at the end of the airfield. Relieved, I watched as they flew over Thyangboche Monastery, dwarfed by the snowy bulk of Taweche, and set course for Katmandu.

We now began preparations for the climax of the expedition, the assault on Makalu. First we had to move more than two hundred loads across the high-level route to the Barun Glacier, where we planned to locate Camp I, the first of the seven camps we would need to climb the mountain. This was a formidable task for the heavily laden Sherpas, who would have to cross the 19,600-foot Ama Dablam Col into the Hongu Valley, then climb to the 20,000-foot Barun plateau, and finally work their way down the difficult route to the great Barun Glacier, below the west face of Makalu.

This was one of the most strenuous periods of the expedi-

The assault on Makalu

Drawing by John Harrison

1. The author, Michael Gill, and Pat Barcham, leaning against rocks inscribed with Nepali.

2. Larry Swan (left) and Marlin Perkins display the skin that Desmond Doig purchased from an aged nun at Beding. To the Sherpas it was definitely that of the Dzu-Teh, a large type of Yeti.

3. Talking to Nepali porter is Bhanu Bannerjee (left), high-caste Bengali who acted as interpreter for Peter Mulgrew.

4. Sir Edmund Hillary.

5. John Harrison.

6. Wally Romanes.

7. Michael Ward.

8. Leigh Ortenberger.

9. Tom Nevison.

10. Dawa Thondup. Ever present and just visible here (on his ancient red balaclava), a small plastic-covered photograph of the Dalai Lama.

11. Annulu, Urkein, and Mingmatsering, expedition sirdars.

12. June Mulgrew with her Sherpas.

13. Dawa Tenzing, described by Desmond Doig as "a patriarchal figure of indeterminate age who exudes personality and alcoholic fumes."

14. Entering a Nepali village on the way to the Everest region.

15. Elder of Khumjung and guardian of the Yeti scalp, Khunjo Chumbi holds Philip Tobgay Chumbi as his wife combs his hair.

16. Lamas from the Khumjung gompa.

tion, and sahibs and Sherpas alike worked long and arduous hours. Camps were established, routes found, and dozens of loads relayed across some of the most desolate and spectacular country in the world. Most mornings the weather was fine and sunny, but by the late afternoons we were usually battling bitter cold and mist, often accompanied by clouds of driven snow.

By April 17, Camp I was established in the lateral trough behind the moraine wall, high above the Barun Glacier. Despite strong, cold winds and frequent snowfalls we kept the relaying program moving. In less than two weeks the last of the loads had come down from the plateau and the camp had expanded to three rock huts and several tents. We now set ourselves to the assault on Makalu and were soon ready to begin the lift to Camps II and III. Extra high-altitude clothing was issued to the Sherpas and 120 loads of assault rations and gear were made ready. Our first aim was to establish a camp on the Makalu Col—a 24,300-foot saddle between the main peak of Makalu, nearly 28,000 feet high, and its northern subsidiary, Makalu II, 25,120 feet high. Apart from the summit itself we expected the route to the col to present the greatest problem, as it was difficult of approach and excessively steep. Camp II was readily established atop a great rock tower near the middle of the Makalu Glacier. This comfortable camp had a magnificent outlook and became easily the most popular camp on Makalu.

So far the route had proved tedious rather than difficult, although one deep gully that was studded with pinnacles of ice proved a menace to the slower-moving Sherpas with their heavy loads. I always got through this place as quickly as I could myself and reached Camp II with relief. Above the camp the route ran along a rib of snow beside the glacier, then up a steep gully crammed full of loose shingle and on toward the foot of a steep ice wall.

John Harrison cut a long string of big bucket steps in the ice wall and installed a fixed rope. Above the wall we found a plane of soft powdery snow covering numerous deep crevasses. Gradually we worked our way through these, marking each one with an orange flag. Wearing crampons and roped together, we plugged away at the slope under the towering rock face of Makalu II for almost three hours, and here, on a gentle ridge between two large crevasses we pitched Camp III at 21,000 feet.

We set up the large dome tent and several four-man tents, consolidating our position and giving ourselves a good roomy advanced base for the next phase, the move to the col. Our first night in Camp III was marred by a storm, with strong winds and heavy, driving snow. Next morning it was clear but still blustery. Harrison, Nevison, and two Sherpas began cutting steps toward a great ice couloir almost directly below the col. Hillary planned to install a fixed rope in the couloir and place Camp IV in some suitable spot between the top of the couloir and the col itself. During the day we were able to catch odd glimpses of Harrison's party pushing on toward the foot of the couloir. They arrived back in camp just before dark, desperately tired but elated. They had found a good route and had put in more than five hundred feet of fixed rope leading right to the very entrance of the couloir.

Next morning Dawa Thondup woke with such a bad headache that I had to tell him to stay in camp. I was almost as disappointed as he was. Annulu took his place alongside Ortenberger and me. We were to carry on with the route begun by Harrison and Nevison.

We climbed up the established steps to the end of the fixed rope. From here into the couloir we found steep solid ice and took some time cutting a safe line of steps. I found this very hard work and was pleased to let the others take their turn. Once into the couloir we had to take extreme care. It was very steep. One serious slip and practically nothing could save us, for the couloir drained out over a thousand feet of ice bluffs. Fortunately it was full of good snow with only a little ice.

We were all relieved to get pitons driven in and begin fixing the rope. Two-thirds of the way up the couloir we branched to the right among some ice cliffs and zigzagged backward and forward to gain height. By late afternoon we were out of the top of the couloir at an altitude of 23,000 feet and ready to turn back. We worked our way slowly down, fixing the last of the rope as we came and improving the steps wherever we could. After nine hours of solid work we were back in Camp III tired but pleased with the day's work. The next day Hillary and Romanes clambered back up the couloir, where they completed the fixed ropes and located Camp IV on an exposed bulge of snow above the couloir.

They returned in thick visibility and steadily falling snow that continued during the night and most of the next day. In spite of this weather Hillary was anxious to push on and establish Camp V on the col. Accordingly Milledge and I set out to re-establish the route up the fixed ropes to Camp IV. We found all the steps completely filled with snow and had a strenuous time making the route once more negotiable. We were closely followed by Ward and Gill with seven tough Sherpas, each carrying forty pounds. Milledge and I helped pitch the tents, then started back for Camp III, leaving Ward and Gill with two Sherpas, ready to attempt the col the next morning.

Snow fell steadily all evening, followed by a tremendous wind that thrashed the tents unmercifully. We were forced to shout at each other to make ourselves heard as the wind roared across the rock ramparts of Makalu II immediately above the camp.

This continuously bad weather was making it hard to keep the route open. Hillary worried that we might all wear ourselves out recutting the snow-filled steps each day. After two days' hard work on the rocks and snow traverse above Camp IV, Ward and Gill reached the col. Hillary was delighted, for the route to the col was now open. All that remained to do was to lift up the bulk of the stores and set up Camp V.

On May 6, Romanes and Harrison spent the day putting in hundreds of feet of rope between Camp IV and the Makalu Col. They worked in shocking weather and in the face of opposition to the use of so much rope, but as later events proved this was a wise precaution. The next day was as usual unpleasant, with heavy snow falling and fierce gusts of wind. Hillary almost decided to have a rest day, but we still had to lift the main quantity of supplies and time was short. This was a vital task, for on its success depended all the future activities of the expedition, and everyone was anxious to see it completed. Hillary asked Ortenberger and me to prepare the loads and suggested that we bring as many Sherpas as possible into play. We were pleased to get on with it, for by now we were fed up with the weather and saw little hope of its clearing for a few days. With twenty-three heavily laden Sherpas we plowed our way up the ice couloir to Camp IV.

Harrison and Romanes, having spent the morning finishing the route above the camp, were just about to leave as we arrived. We gathered outside the tents talking for a few minutes, but it was too cold and windy to stand about for long and Ortenberger and I were anxious for the warmth of our sleeping bags.

We could see little of the surrounding mountains for windblown snow, but as darkness came the wind dropped, and it began to snow heavily. With the aid of sleeping tablets we slept moderately well and woke before dawn, dismayed to hear the wind battering the tents as badly as ever. A thick white carpet of packed snow covered the twenty-three loads, and we were some time getting them clear. In crowded conditions, with the attendant difficulties of eating, the Sherpas made a slow start, but finally we were away. The wind had lessened a little, which was a help, but it was bitterly cold and miserable for the Sherpas, who traveled slowly with their heavy loads.

Only a hundred yards or so above the camp two Sherpas stopped and resolutely refused to go on. They had both vomited and were suffering from headaches, so with no alternative I took one or two vital items from their loads and sent them back. Ortenberger was now away ahead, leading the first of the Sherpas up the fixed ropes below the col. I hurried to catch up, cursing the weather and blowing like a wounded whale. We were all feeling the altitude, and I for one was very grateful for the ropes Harrison had fixed. Clipped to them with a karabiner or using them for hauling myself up, I found them invaluable, and although the rocks were steep and icy I felt secure. By the time I reached the lip of the col most of the Sherpas were already over, dumping their loads on a patch of scree among some ice waves and crouching behind them for shelter. The wind hit me with such force that I had to bend double for a few yards and crawl. Ortenberger had already started sending Sherpas down, and as soon as the last of the loads was in and everything checked we turned back ourselves.

I had never been this high before, and reaching the col was a great thrill to me, although I had almost no chance to look about.

I knew that we were now in Tibet proper, for the border runs right through the center of Makalu. Through the flying snow showers I caught glimpses of brown plains and distant peaks, but I was really much too cold to appreciate the surroundings. Like the Sherpas I was primarily interested in starting down again away from the wind.

From the edge of the col I could see figures strung out along the fixed rope, heading enthusiastically for Camp IV. Even the two sick Sherpas had come part way up the slope to meet them, as pleased as we were with the success of the carry.

We arrived at Camp III during the late afternoon. It was snowing and we were tired, but we had the satisfaction of a job well done, and personally I was pleased with myself at reaching the col without undue fatigue. Tom Nevison had tea ready for us, but before I could start to drink he startled us both with the disturbing news that Hillary had suffered what Tom called "a cerebral vascular accident." Nevison was not sure how serious the stroke was, as the news had been indistinctly passed to him by radio from Camp II. I waited impatiently for the evening "sked" and was much relieved to hear Camp II come on loud and clear. Ed had moved down to the more sustaining altitudes of Camp I, with Jim Milledge to look after him and keep him company. By all reports he was much improved but would probably have to be flown out. I was appalled to hear this, as I knew that he would never permit himself to be evacuated unless he were very sick indeed.

Worried by this unexpected turn of events, I passed a restless night and determined at first light that I would set out for Camp I. With luck I could breakfast at Camp II, then push on to be in Camp I around midday.

Fresh snow had obliterated all signs of the route, but I was able to make good progress by following the bamboo poles spaced at intervals between Camp III and the glacier above Camp II. Traveling alone, I took great care for the first three-quarters of an hour, as there were many partly concealed crevasses sprinkled across the now invisible trail.

Once clear of these and on sound ice, I speeded up and soon caught sight of the tents of Camp II perched among the rocks above the glacier. Someone waved and in no time I was crowded into the tent with John Harrison, Mike Ward, John West, and Wally Romanes. Mike Gill, having one of his periodic attacks of "gut rot," was sitting miserably in his sleeping bag writing letters.

They were in touch by radio with Ed, who told them that he had handed over direction of the assault to Mike Ward, the most experienced Himalayan climber among us. Hillary's general plans were on paper, so the organization would be his, although Ward was left to make any decision he chose once the assault was under way. I learned that the two assault parties were to consist of Romanes, Harrison, and Gill in the first assault, and Ward, Nevison, Ortenberger, and myself in the second. I must confess that I was disappointed at missing the chance to go with the first three, who were New Zealanders and who would, I felt certain, climb the mountain.

However, they were clearly the stronger climbers in the party and the obvious choice for the first attempt. Also they were now rested after their few days' relaxation at Camp II, and we had all noticed how quickly one becomes stale and dilatory at high altitudes without any break.

I was soon away again in company with Mingma Tsering, Ed's personal Sherpa, whose main concern was to be with the Burra Sahib now that he was sick. Mingma was greatly attached to Hillary, and although as anxious to climb Makalu as we were, he intended to give up his chances and if necessary go out to Katmandu with him. I felt much the same way. Since our years together in the antarctic a strong friendship had developed between us, and for me the sting would be lost from the expedition if he were no longer there.

Although Ward had assured me that it was not likely provided he remained at low altitude, I had the nagging fear that Ed might have another attack, perhaps fatal, and I could never had forgiven myself if I had been away on the mountain when I might have been some help. These thoughts passed through my mind as Mingma and I hurriedly picked our way down the boulder-strewn glacier toward Camp I.

I remembered a remark Griff Pugh made a few weeks before as we discussed the complexities of leading such a mixed bunch of nationalities and built-in prejudices in the Himalayas. "The whole thing is simple as far as you are concerned," he said. "An instruction is given and years of naval training compel you, almost without conscious thought, to carry it out. You see the leader as a captain and yourself as crew and no momentary hesitation clouds your view."

Unaccountably Gilbert's lines ran through my head, "He never thought of thinking for himself at all." This uncompromising attitude of Pugh's is based on a common misconception of service discipline and is in fact only partly true. I felt that no leader, no matter how competent, could hope to gain his objective if he were bogged by argument and trivialities of direction and organization. If he is good enough to lead, then in my view common loyalty should suffice those fortunate enough to accompany him.

Sometimes the prospective expeditioner will make any sacrifice and agree at home to any program, but once he is in the field his good intentions evaporate and he becomes embroiled in trivia and divided loyalties. Loyalty, some say, is the last refuge of the incompetent, but I see it, as does Lord Cobham, "the cardinal virtue."

Of course, on an expedition everyone is an individual; he would, in all probability, not be there if he were not. Some are strongly competitive; others are easier in outlook but as determined. In a mixed expedition some have national characteristics that may in time tend to grate, while others have simple quirks of temperament that must needs be considered in the everyday routine of expedition life. The leader must hold these men, bound by some common will and imbued with the same purposeful spirit that he himself imparts to the enterprise.

I believe that the loyalty and determination engendered by men such as Shackleton and Franklin stemmed from their own immense qualities as leaders, and one such of this select group, I hold, is Sir John Hunt; another, Sir Edmund Hillary. There are those, it is true, who do not share this view of Hillary, but I notice they are rarely men who know him well and are more often those who seem driven by an unreasonable and compelling jealousy to castigate any public figure or popular hero. Perhaps this is not surprising, as the very strength of his nature makes him enemies as well as friends. Fortuitous circumstance, some say, placed him on the summit of Everest— "It might have been anyone." Those who have experienced his formidable determination and turbulent energy doubt it. Like George Lowe, they feel that he was the right man, possibly the only man, in the right place at the right time.

Edmund Percival Hillary is a complex person with a depth of character which few people discern from a casual meeting. There is nothing flamboyant about him, absolutely no showmanship, and, at least on the surface, he is no textbook hero. Indeed he can be scornful of the more romantic conceptions of mountaineering. All the same it is probable that, in their profound sincerity, his own conceptions of exploration and climbing mountains are the most romantic of all. To this man adventure itself, and the ability of man by physical and moral training to conquer the erstwhile impossible, are the basic ingredients of life.

He is not a demonstrative person—credit and praise from him are never misplaced and are infinitely more valuable than the same sentiment expressed by the garrulous. Family life is very important to him, he is devoted to his own. And one senses in him a deep moral conviction, essentially old-fashioned and sometimes even prim. He belies an apparent vanity by a disarming facility for self-criticism. He may not know all his own weaknesses, but is quite unresentful of criticism. Running as it does like so much water from the back of the long-suffering proverbial duck, criticism does not get time to sink in, much less bear fruit.

He hates the gushing, the fawning, and that constant lack of anonymity that must accompany such people as himself, but he accepts it all now as unavoidable. He is a man of balanced judgment and real friendliness, yet he can appear surprisingly thoughtless, even careless of the feelings of others. He is always ready to assist those not as well known as

himself in adventurous pursuits, and he invariably includes
young New Zealanders in his own expeditions.

Americans are tremendously impressed by his acknowledged organizing ability, but above this they say that he
stands out as being a "refreshingly decent man." He has been
described as "a virtuoso, deeply and constantly embroiled in
his art." Like Peter Paul Rubens, "he is a truly golden character."

Ed was pleased to see Mingma and me when we arrived
at his tent shortly after midday. His speech was slightly
slurred and he was a little unsteady on his feet, but otherwise there was no other outward sign of what must have
been a terrifying experience. He told me that it had all
started with a headache.

He had arrived at Camp II feeling unwell, with a miserable pain on the left side of his forehead and face. During
the afternoon he slept, to be awakened by a Sherpa bringing
the evening meal. The pain in the side of his head and face
had now intensified and he was unable to get the Sherpa to
understand him. He felt helpless, divorced from his limbs,
and, although able to think quite clearly, spoke gibberish
whenever he tried to say anything.

Mike Ward and Jim Milledge in a nearby tent heard him
and, quickly realizing the position, put him on oxygen for
the night and gave him some pain-relieving drugs. The following morning Mike Ward insisted that he go down, at
least below 15,000 feet, and stay down. Hillary was far from
enthusiastic about this but did not struggle too hard, as he
still felt decidedly seedy. He walked down to Camp I without help, and next day, the day Mingma and I arrived, he
was feeling much better.

He hastily put an end to efforts to have him flown out to
Katmandu by helicopter, but agreed to return via the Barun
Valley, the low-level route, to Khumjung. Mingma Tsering

and I were both anxious to abandon the mountain and return with him, but he would not hear of it.

I greatly admired Jim Milledge, who never hesitated in his determination to remain with Hillary. Jim was as keen as the rest of us to go high on Makalu, especially as his prime interest lay in the physiological aspects of high-altitude work, but he felt that, as a doctor first and foremost, he must stay with Hillary.

In a vain attempt to relieve Milledge's conscience and persuade him to return to the climb, we sent a message to Captain Motwani, still at base camp in the Mingbo Valley. We suggested that he gather some Sherpas and cross the Ama Dablam Col and the Hongu plateau as quickly as possible, meet Hillary in the Barun Valley, and accompany him back to Khumjung. Motwani, a big, strong, bearded Indian doctor, was attached to the expedition from the Indian Army. Apart from being about the hugest man in the party he was among the best-qualified for a Himalayan expedition. Medical background aside, he was a graduate of the Indian mountaineering school at Darjeeling, where he had passed with honors. He was also a member designate of the coming Indian Everest expedition. He was bright and cheerful and invariably ate heartily, but he seemed to lack some essential ingredient—drive, dedication, determination, call it what you will. Nothing would persuade Motwani to cross the Hongu.

By radio that evening Tom Nevison pointed out that the first assault party was an all-New Zealand one, and, while this was of little concern among ourselves, it might be misconstrued by the American public. Hillary, who was more interested in performance than nationalities, conceded the point and asked John Harrison and Leigh Ortenberger to change places. This was unfortunate for Harrison, who had acclimatized exceedingly rapidly and who was undoubtedly one of the strong men of the party.

On the morning of May 10, Mingma and I left Hillary and

Milledge and began the long grind back to Camp II. For us the assault had begun.

By May 12, Harrison and I were enjoying beautiful weather at Camp III. Earlier in the day, apparently miles above us, we saw the little black dots of the first assault party moving leisurely up the fixed ropes from Camp IV to the col.

As the first summit attempt progressed above us, Harrison and I moved on toward Camp V, on the col. We were little bothered by the wind, although we could see sheets of snow blowing from the upper reaches of the mountain and wondered how the others were faring in the obviously unpleasant weather higher up.

Our respite was not to last for long. As we breasted the col we were hit by violent gusts of wind and were glad to seek the shelter of the large Blanchard tent pitched among a lot of mushrooming *sastrugi*.

Ward, West, and Nevison were in residence and had the scientific work in full swing. Since leaving Camp IV, I had found difficulty in keeping my hands warm, and now in the pleasant fug of the Blanchard they ached miserably as the circulation returned.

That night the wind blew, buffeting the tent so much that I was unable to sleep, and driving fine snow through the tightly laced tent flaps. We worried about Romanes and party, who were due to make the summit attempt the next day. At 8 A.M. we turned on the radio intending to call Desmond Doig at the Silver Hut before moving on to Camp VI. We were amazed to hear the summit party come on the air and tell us that they were back at Camp VI and about to leave for Camp V. Not only had they had no chance to attempt the summit, but they were apparently in full flight after a terrific beating from the fierce winds above the col. All we could do was wait patiently until they returned to hear the full story. About midday they came in, absolutely exhausted, covered in frost and utterly beaten. Mike Gill was the worst hit, with an ugly-looking frostbite on his nose and cheeks and complaints of grittiness behind his eyes, a fore-warning of snow blindness.

Romanes was little better, although he had escaped frost-bite. He and Gill on the leading rope had born the brunt of the hard work, cutting all the steps and forcing a way through the ice seracs above Camp VI. Ortenberger, though tired, had been able to save himself a good deal and seemed in reasonable condition. Gill and Romanes were clearly finished and would probably have to go down. Although they had been forced to turn back much earlier than expected, they achieved two things that would be of inestimable value to the second assault team. Firstly, they had safely installed Camp VI, and secondly they had dumped a tent and cooker at 26,300 feet, only 700 feet below the proposed Camp VII. They were finally driven back by bitter winds, their faces caked with ice and their goggles completely frozen up.

On the homeward journey they had been lucky to escape serious injury when a tired Gill slipped on the hard ice and dragged Romanes off his belay. They both tumbled down some fifty feet and ended up half buried in the snow below. Fortunately they were unhurt and managed to drag themselves the last few steps to Camp VI.

Romanes felt that their downfall had come about mainly through their underestimating the effect of wind and altitude on men already weakened by shortage of oxygen. They had worn themselves out cutting steps and forcing a route through the glacier seracs above Camp VI. He advised us to save ourselves as much as possible in readiness for the terrible strain we would be subjected to above 27,000 feet.

Romanes also suggested that we endeavor to improve the route through the seracs, an area that he thought would present our only real technical difficulty. With this in mind and the possibility of the second assault also meeting unexpected difficulties, Ward decided to keep Harrison and himself, together with a strong team of Sherpas, in reserve. They would follow a day behind Annulu, Nevison, and me, who were to extend the route through the seracs, install Camp VII, and then attempt the summit if the weather continued to hold.

The stricken state of Romanes and Gill had impressed upon me how rigorous climbing in such conditions really was, and I must confess that the prospect of facing these conditions without oxygen caused me some concern at this stage. Not that I thought about giving up or returning—I was as keen as ever—but a change had occurred. No longer did I view the climb as a wonderful opportunity, a glorious mountaineering holiday afforded me by beneficent circumstance.

Above the col we found nature not only at her most magnificent but also at her most elemental. Here we were almost unconscious of the splendid visions about us. The grandeur and majesty of the surrounding peaks were as nothing to the deadly weariness that assailed our muscles and drained strength from our ambition. Above all, the wind was always with us, a constant background to our thoughts during the day and an insidious penetration of our dreams at night, wind so bereft of every quality of life and gentleness and so intensely cold that it froze the very marrow in our bones.

More than six miles high we lived in a gray world, one so different from that vital world in which men normally live and breathe that we might just as well have been the inhabitants of a strange and distant planet.

"Surely the gods live here, beaten down by the silence and the appalling sweep and dispersal of the cloud shadows after rain. This is no place for men." These lines of Rudyard Kipling are the most nearly adequate description for the uncanny atmosphere of this place—an atmosphere part physical, part spiritual.

SEVEN

Advance to the Summit

Great things are done when men and mountains meet,
This is not done by jostling in the street.

William Blake

AT EARLIEST LIGHT the wind was blowing as strongly as ever, but now for the first time in several days the great rock rib below the sharp peak of Makalu was clearly visible. Even from more than 24,000 feet the summit plume streaming across the icy Tibetan uplands drifted like a gigantic pale pennant marking our ultimate goal, still so far beyond our reach.

It was not necessary to make an early start, for it was our intention on this, the first day of the assault, to spend the night at Camp VI. It had already been established and would need only a little snow-clearing work to make it habitable.

Nevison and I, after a reassuring look at the weather, lost no time in retiring to our still-warm sleeping bags, where we sipped lemon tea and discussed endless plans for the assault. Annulu, brave soul, had already begun to check the prepared loads, working with his back to the wind as casually as though he were making his Sunday *tsampa* at Thyangboche.

As we talked, John West emerged from his sleeping bag and with characteristic enthusiasm began to perform what at first appeared to be a strange and mystic ceremony. Ignoring our inquiries, he took several deep breaths, triumphantly turned a delicate shade of purple, and blew into a glass bulb, closing the stopper with the air of a master magician. Somewhat exhausted, he was soon revived with a draught of lemon tea, being pleased to explain that in the "trade" this was known as alveolar air collecting and represented his last performance at 24,000 feet. He and Mike Ward having completed the physiological program, John now intended to return to Camp III, Mike to remain and direct the assault.

"For an Australian," as John Harrison remarked with a laugh, and a person with almost no mountaineering experience, John West had far exceeded both his own and Hillary's expectations. He had tackled the difficult climb up to Camp V with the assurance of a born mountaineer and in addition seemed one of those least affected by the altitude. Conscientious to the point of fatigue, West was an immensely hardworking and popular member of the team.

The wind had by no means dropped, but had lost much of its former venom. Even so the brilliant orange flags marking the edge of the col whipped and cracked as the wind, furiously tugging at our tents, hurled showers of vaporized snow at the distant Tibetan plateau thousands of feet below.

I crossed to one of the small Mead tents where Mike Gill, as yet not recovered from the first assault, lay in his sleeping bag. He was still very tired, his face was burned from the combination of sun and wind, and his frostbitten cheeks and nose gave mute evidence of his recent ordeal.

No sense in waiting further, we thought, the wind will not drop much more, and we may well need the extra time at Camp VI, where the tents would probably need repitching.

With a round of "good lucks" and a few words on the assault from Mike Ward, Tom Nevison and I were on our way. The start was a chilly one, but we soon warmed to our work with many new steps to cut and almost all the old ones to clear of snow. Ice crystals, instantly licked up by the wind, flew stingingly into Annulu's face as he brought on the second rope of Sherpas but a few steps below.

We made a long traverse, climbing steadily toward a jumble of rocks straggling down the center of the ice field. Now

27,790'

x 27,400'

⑦ 27,000'

⑥ⁱ

SHERPA SLIP

⑥ 25,800'

⑤ 24,300'

Mount Makalu: Detail of routes above Camp V

Drawing by John Harrison

and again the snow-filled steps cut by the returning first assault party appeared faintly on the windswept hard green ice, almost as though some mysterious biped had just stepped out the route in front of us, remaining always out of sight—

hidden in the patches of mist and wind-driven snow scurrying around the mountain.

Tom and I rested briefly at the rock outcrop as the Sherpas moved slowly toward Camp VI, now visible as a yellow splash against the massive ice towers of the upper Makalu Glacier. Camp VI was certainly no place for the imaginative. Immediately above the tents a monumental ice bulge promised the loss of the whole party should it decide to take its natural course and sweep down the mountain. As far as I could see it would have been difficult to pick a worse spot for a camp, but I was bound to say that I could see none better in the immediate vicinity.

We pushed on but were now definitely feeling the altitude. Each upward step was an increasing effort, while the need for careful cramponing and rope management required a mental concentration almost as tiring as the physical.

The final five hundred feet to Camp VI steepened rapidly, coming to an abrupt stop where our two tents were perched on the crest of a small snow platform. Soon I could see Hakpa Norbu Khundi's brown face peering over the rim, hugely enjoying the humiliating wheezing sound I made as I labored up the slope.

I was finding it hard going and was a little disappointed at the modest pace I was forced to set. Tom seemed as fit as ever and once in camp set about helping to clear the snow from within the partly collapsed tents. We soon had a brew going and I passed on a progress report by radio to Camp V, in return receiving a somewhat incoherent reply from Mike Ward. We were now at 25,800 feet, and here we decided to leave the nine-pound radio.

Fully clothed and snugly bedded down in our double sleeping bags, things began to look rather rosy. With good weather the next day we confidently expected to establish Camp VII and so be in a good position for a shot at the summit. Even if the weather or our physical condition should stop us from making the attempt, the successful installation of Camp VII would give the last assault party, Harrison and Ortenberger, a much better chance for their try.

Uncomforted by Nevison's remark that "the advantage of sleeping below a mammoth ice block is that it gives safety from avalanches"—the theory being that the snow would flow around each side of the camp—I dreamed fitfully of the weight of snow forcing the monster ice mass to lose its grip and press us neatly into space, to arrive in Tibet 12,000 feet later, closely followed by an ice block the size of a battle-ship.

Conscious that this would probably be our most vital and difficult day, we were away early. There was little hope that our assault party or those who followed would reach the top unless we could put the next camp as high as possible. This meant at least to 27,000 feet or more, an extremely difficult feat without the use of oxygen. From this exposed position our gaze passed at a glance over inconceivable distances. Still the wind blew, but now everything was miraculously clear. A savage mountain world, a world remote from all human preoccupations, lay before us, the peaks standing out of the shadows of the glaciers like flaming spires slowly turning crimson in the early sun.

With the exception of Annulu we planned, once Camp VII was established, to send the five remaining Sherpas back alone to the col. With this in mind Ward had asked us to improve the route as much as possible and where necessary to provide fixed ropes.

With the wind cold at our backs we were soon busy securing the first rope from within a few yards of the camp over a difficult ice pitch. As well we did, for had this rope not been there on the return journey I would certainly never have got off the mountain. Once this was done we were into the small glacier dividing the northern face of Makalu and lying between us and the highest point reached by Romanes. Here his party had dumped the tent for Camp VII before returning.

Nevison and I felt fairly fit but had learned a lesson from the first assault, when the two strongest sahibs had exhausted themselves doing the majority of the work. We left much of the step cutting or clearing to the Sherpas, who were now led on ahead by Annulu. Driving pitons and fixing ropes in certain places, we sahibs made steady progress, although in time falling a little behind the Sherpas, who were going very well. Two or three times we made long traverses to avoid seracs, taking care to lose as little height as possible in the process. Each foot of altitude had been too hard won to be readily given up, were there any other way round the obstacle.

After three and a half hours of not overly strenuous work we were across the bulk of the glacier and close, we thought, to the spot where the dump had been left. We were both in excellent spirits. I was over my lethargy of the previous day and now felt stronger than ever before.

The string of Sherpas, with Annulu still in the lead, reached the point where he supposed the supplies had been dumped, by now, of course, well buried by the drifting snow. As Tom Nevison and I rounded the last of the broken glacier ice, we saw the Sherpas strung out across the snow face, each firm in his crampons but none belaying, while Annulu probed around with his ax in the hard-packed snow.

Then suddenly, to our horror, at the end of the line Da Tenzing II stooped on the steep and treacherous slope intending to take up the tension on his crampon strap. He momentarily lost his balance and slipped, both legs shooting from under him as he fell backward down the slope.

Within seconds each of the five other Sherpas found himself plucked in turn off the mountain face and unwillingly hurled down the slope after his companions, completely unable to check his descent.

It happened suddenly and seemingly without noise. Each man was tugged off the mountain like a puppet on a string. Before we could yell a warning the rope reached Annulu, who was still digging industriously. Just as he straightened up he too found himself plucked into the air.

As Tom and I watched, powerless to make a move, the Sherpas fell, slowly at first but soon with a rapidly increasing momentum, directly toward a serrated ice bulge bridging the narrow trough, down which they slid to certain death. None could stop himself; by now three had lost their ice axes and so their main hope of escape. Shedding loads as they fell, they sped on in an untidy heap toward the sheer northern wall of the Makalu massif. Once over that there was practically a free drop of several thousand feet onto the Tibetan plateau.

In shocked silence we watched as they shot over the ice bulge, turning in the air amid flying packs, axes, and miscellaneous items of clothing, to crash finally onto the slope running to the edge of the last horrifying drop. Then all was changed, as though a miracle had happened. The ice face at this point was pitted by narrow, subtly concealed crevasses lightly bridged with snow. By the greatest of good fortune the last two men on the rope, Annulu and Hakpa Norbu, fell through a snow bridge into a fairly shallow crevasse. The six had been falling in a long, straggling line, like an untidily knotted length of string. With Annulu and Hakpa Norbu disappearing into the crevasse the rope was caused to tighten and fortunately hold; biting into the snow on the lower wall, it brought the remaining Sherpas to a sudden halt amid a flurry of fine powdered snow.

Nevison and I were left high above our companions. Sick at heart, we could see three of them lying in the snow as though dead. In vertical height they had fallen perhaps six hundred feet, but the distance covered across the steep slope would probably have ended up at more than a thousand feet.

We immediately began to cut our way down, but it was a slow and difficult task across hard green ice, collecting scattered equipment as we descended. Only two Sherpas had apparently moved since the fall, and our hearts were heavy as we examined them, taking care to secure each by their still miraculously unbroken rope to an ax driven deep in the snow. These two, Mingma Tsering and Ang Temba, were terribly dazed, both sitting immobile in the snow in an obviously shocked state. A long, unheeded trickle of blood ran down Mingma's face, splashing his legs and staining the snow around him. Annulu and his companion had by now managed to extricate themselves from the crevasse, with the aid of Annulu's ax, which he had determinedly retained. With Annulu's help we collected everyone together and after an examination found to our intense surprise that, apart from the severe shake-up, only two Sherpas seemed to be hurt at all, and they not really badly. Ang Temba had sprained his leg but could still walk, and Mingma had cut his head and face on flying crampons.

What were we to do? The two injured Sherpas would obviously have to return to Base Camp, but if the whole party now turned about without putting in the highest camp, all chance of climbing Makalu would be lost. Without the Camp VII tents in position Harrison and Ortenberger could never hope to carry enough food and fuel, especially with the sadly depleted team of Sherpas now remaining on the col at Camp V.

The Sherpas soon began to rally, still much subdued but buoyed by the lack of serious injury among themselves. Mingma Tsering, taking a brave stand, insisted that he was "much estrong," although it was clear that he would have to go down. With the decision made that Mingma and Ang Temba should return we put it to the others to elect, forward or retreat. We had no intention of trying to force the issue after the terrifying ordeal they had just been through. They must all show certain signs of wanting to go on, or we should inevitably return.

"Providing we do not have to carry the extra loads left by the two injured men," said Annulu, "on we will go."

This was certainly not unreasonable, as they knew that they still had to collect the food and equipment that was scattered when the accident happened. It was plain to Nevison and me that we could no longer conserve our energies for the "summit day." To go on, we must be prepared to carry some of the load ourselves. Finally I agreed to take the bulk of the loads, consisting of a tent, a cooker, and some food packs. Nevison, with only his ice ax, felt that he could safely lead and take responsibility for doing all the cutting and plugging necessary to get us to 27,000 feet, where we intended to site Camp VII.

Fortunately the wind had lessened; a weak sun shone from a tiny patch of blue sky. Gradually the patch broadened, and the sun, feeling its strength, burst through. Laboriously and with great caution we began the reascent to the depot. We climbed roped, taking particular note of the several concealed crevasses.

Relieved to be once more on the move and active, we soon had the depot dug out and the various loads re-sorted. Here the two injured men began the return journey, both much recovered and confident. We congratulated ourselves on the wonderful spirit of our Sherpas as we watched them cross the glacier, blessing the fixed ropes, now so vital.

From the depot a broad ice rib ran toward the summit, splitting the face in two. We knew that the 1955 French expedition had taken the left side of this rib, up a narrow, snow-filled channel. Full of fine powdery snow and under overhanging ice cliffs, it looked too dangerous to us. Lacking the strength which the Frenchmen, using oxygen, had had in reserve, we chose the other side, which was a steep but less hazardous snow field.

We were desperately tired after the exertions of the last few hours, and at this high altitude it felt almost a physical impossibility to force enough air into our laboring lungs. No matter how often we paused for breath there seemed to be little nourishment in the air. We were frequently forced to halt, wind-blown and prostrate, trying to gather enough power to raise our spiked high-altitude boots for the next short step. Gradually we kicked our way into a snow couloir —a narrow three-hundred-foot furrow in the mountainside —straining and blowing with every step.

Tom's face, occasionally visible between his legs as I toiled directly below him, had turned a vivid purple, with diffused red patches splotching through it, giving him a strange and personal aura. I had no doubt that I appeared equally curious, and wondered how the Sherpas' brown faces now looked after the floury color they had managed to turn following their fall.

During one of our numerous stops in the couloir the Sherpas used valuable breath in enthusiasm over the delights of a campsite right where we were—oblivious of the fact that we were perched on a precipitous slope with no prospect of securing a level area for tents, and with the surety of becoming air-borne should the few inches of snow adhering to the steep surface decide to avalanche.

The Sherpas had obviously had enough and were anxious to return hard on the heels of their injured companions, who, we hoped, had now reached Camp VI.

I was determined to set up the tents as close to the 27,000-foot mark as possible in order to make the final day's climb short enough to ensure a reasonable chance of success. In addition we needed to leave enough time after we reached the campsite to allow the Sherpas to complete their return journey. Already the sun was falling toward the South Col of Everest, now clearly visible over the white shoulder of Makalu. There was no time to be lost.

Above us and to the left ran the exposed lip of a good-sized bergschrund, a crevasse dividing the snow field on which we were standing from the summit pyramid. We set out once again, Tom leading and I coming on behind, enlarging the steps and blowing like a grampus. No one spoke; each was concentrating on forcing every ounce of energy into mak-

17. The rare view of the Everest region, seen from the Tesi Lapcha. Left to right, the summit of Everest, south col, Nuptse, and the sharp peak of Lhotse.

18. Crossing the Tesi Lapcha. Making for the bottom of the pass, the men spread out to move in small groups with others from their own village. The Namche Bazaar Sherpas usually took a positive delight in being as slow as possible.

19. Makalu col and summit taken from the air in 1945 by Squadron Leader Cliff Andrews.

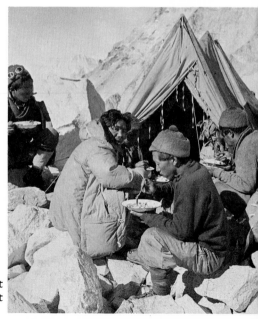

20. Camp II. Sherpa breakfast at the most secure and most popular campsite.

21. Camp V on the col.

22. The climb above Camp V. "Now and again the snow-filled steps cut by the returning first assault party appeared faintly on the windswept hard green ice . . ."

23. Camp VI. "No place for the imaginative. . . . I dreamed fitfully of the weight of snow forcing the monster ice globule to loose its grip and press us neatly into space."

24. "Get up and take a few more steps, get up and take a few more steps."

ing the next step. With agonizing slowness we reached the bergschrund, eyes bulging and hearts pounding as we took the last few steps, to collapse on the narrow ledge and lie exhausted for fully ten or fifteen minutes. Once recovered, the eager Sherpas, with the exception of Annulu, were off and soon could be seen strung out on the slope below, getting smaller and smaller as they disappeared down the couloir back to Camp VI.

A reading of our altimeters showed that we had stopped just a little above 27,000 feet. This pleased us very much and we congratulated Annulu, who grinned happily as Tom showed him the height on the altimeter scale.

The day was late, the snows no longer so harsh, white, and glaring. Already dusk had begun to steal from the valleys, long flat blue shadows revealing every undulation of the Barun plateau. Annulu rose heavily to his feet, his ax dragging tiredly as he crossed to the bergschrund and began clearing a platform for the tents. Nevison and I followed. One moment we had been sitting at ease, fully appreciating the magnificent view spread out before us; the next moment we were gasping for air, the simple effort of rising sending our hearts pounding like a hundred hammers. We had forgotten that we were breathing the thin air of over 27,000 feet, where every movement must be made in slow time, giving the heart a chance to handle the enormous extra strain.

At much cost to our failing reserves of energy we prepared the site, pushing surplus snow and ice into the open mouth of the bergschrund. I was not happy, camped hard against the edge of the crevasse, but there was no alternative; around us the mountain fell away at an acute angle, glazed with ice and no easy task to cut at this altitude.

We pitched the tents with their ends butted together so that there was no need to go outside when moving from one to the other. Annulu got the propane cooker going and soon had snow melted for a much-needed mug of lemon tea. I slipped into my capacious double sleeping bag, blessing it for its ease of access, even though I was fully dressed. Insinuating oneself into a tightly fitting bag at high altitude is no joke, and Hillary had designed ours with this in mind.

As we sat talking and sipping tea, I inwardly congratulated myself as I reflected how well we three seemed to be going, especially Annulu, who had suffered an extraordinarily long and trying day. It is true that he had earlier complained of a pain in his chest, but he appeared fit enough now and gave promise of great strength for the morrow.

We drank as much liquid as possible and indeed had taken care to do so since the expedition began. Griff Pugh had many times warned us of the dangers of dehydration; we were only too anxious to take liquid whenever possible. Although there was plenty of freeze-dried meat and fruit in the high-altitude food packs, all we could manage to eat was a little biscuit and jam, washed down with several cups of very sweet tea.

We were now less than eight hundred feet from the summit of Makalu, and by what we could see of the remainder of the climb no great physical difficulty seemed to stand in our way. Providing we remained in good condition, everything would now depend on the weather.

There was little room to move around the camp. With the tents pitched close to the edge of the bergschrund, Nevison even had difficulty finding a place to perch for photography. Although not the most ideal spot, it was probably one of the few safe places for a camp on the upper reaches of the mountain.

I wondered if our little yellow tents could be seen from Camp V and what the others were doing at this moment—probably pedaling their infernal stationary bicycle for test purposes or blowing some of West's multitudinous alveolar air samples.

But I was wrong, as it turned out. Far below us they were having their own troubles: Mike Ward had found it

necessary to use oxygen and Romanes and Gill had returned
to Camp III, exhausted after the tremendous amount of step
cutting and snow plugging they had done during the first
assault.

Huge clouds, sun-crested above, purple-shadowed below,
boiled up from the Barun Valley. Cumulus-girdled subsidiary
peaks were soon lost to view, but Everest, from below the
Lhotse face, stood clear; the sun, falling behind the northern
ridge, threw a golden pathway between us and the South
Col. Incredibly, an army could have maneuvered on the South
Col. In my mind it had always been a narrow, windswept
place with little room for men or tents. But there before me
lay a great rock and snow platform with space for a hundred
tents and as many men. Almost the whole of the successful
British route was visible, from the col to the South Summit;
a broken jagged ridge curved on up to the highest point on
earth, still almost two thousand feet above our camp.

My old friend Ed Hillary, with Tenzing, had reached that
point more than eight years before. Hillary was by now making his slow way down the Barun Valley, I supposed, morti-
fied that for the second time he had been turned back on
Makalu and from almost the same spot on each occasion.
Nevison and I discussed Hillary's illness while Annulu shook
his head sadly, muttering, "Burra Sahib much sick." Hillary
is very popular with all the Sherpa people, held in awe by
many of the villagers and regarded with unbounded affection
by our senior Sherpas, many of whom had climbed with him
on other expeditions. What wouldn't we have given to have
had him with us now, poised for tomorrow's great adventure.

We had an increased respect for the men who climbed
Everest. Now viewed in its true perspective, the summit ridge
looked longer and much steeper than seen from Khumbu.
The route showed some cornicing, and huge blocks of gra-
nitic stone barred the way.

The sun crept behind the glistening white dome of Pumori,
plunging Everest into gloom and leaving the South Col

dreary and chilling, a vast, deserted amphitheater. Briefly, I regretted the loss of my camera, which had gone, along with other personal gear, when the Sherpas had plunged down the mountain. For a moment the distant Tibetan highlands glowed a fiery crimson cape spread over the great plateau, the extended arms touching the golden top of the God King's palace in distant Lhasa. Looking down from the edge of our eyrie, we could see that our companions two and a half thousand feet below had now lost the sun. Quickly and silently the edge of darkness raced toward us.

Tom reached for the candle while I laced up the tent flap, which even now had stiffened in the brisk night air. A stream of freezing vapor forced its way past me into the warmth of the tent, leaving a trace of moisture on my exposed beard. "*Cha hai*, Peter Sahib," from Annulu. Night had come.

We ate little but drank quantities of lemon drink and tea, using the liquid to wash down a few biscuits. Even the freeze-dried fruit and the small blocks of sweet fudge, normally so highly prized, did not tempt the palate. Before long the three of us were tucked well into our double down sleeping bags, the thin air gathering about us, probing with icy fingers for unguarded spots, to form a frosty coating over our tents and persons. Sleep came reluctantly; we dozed for short periods in a fitful and unrestful manner. Toward morning I looked out to find the stars, fiercely brilliant at this altitude, in a pitch-dark sky. There was little wind. Occasionally the distant roar of an avalanche shook the tents slightly. In the lower camps we had sleeping tablets, but above 24,000 feet drugs were not used against the chance that they might produce some abnormal effect.

We had no hope of making a start in the sun, as our camp was deep in shadow and would remain so until well after nine that morning. It was bitterly cold; even our morning cup of tea did little to help, as the boiling point of water at that altitude was reduced to about sixty degrees centigrade.

I struggled into my heavy down jacket, crawling outside

to lace up my boots and put on my crampons. It was miserable work, a case of doing up a strap, then blowing on my lightly gloved hands or putting them under my armpits to warm up again. I worked away for some time, finally getting my boots comfortable, then flinging my arms about to keep the circulation going.

As Nevison prepared the rope, I looked at my watch preparatory to making some notes in my personal log. Surprised, I realized that although we had arisen at 6:15 A.M. it was now just 9:00 o'clock and we were barely ready. I had not been conscious of the passage of time, but obviously we were more anoxic than we realized and were abnormally slowed in the thin air.

I took more careful notice and saw that Tom was needing to rest after making up only a few coils of rope. Every movement required infinitely more effort than at sea level and took at least three times as long.

We must hurry and move off; time was already pressing. I clipped the knotted rope to my shoulder sling and cut a few shallow steps up to the edge of the bergschrund. Annulu and Nevison joined me. In front of us lay a narrow snow bridge with an almost vertical six-foot ice wall behind. I began to doubt my ability to scale it. We cast about and finally found a less steep route, and Annulu was soon on top, belaying while Nevison and I crawled our way up to lie gasping in the soft snow. I had one frozen hand, which Annulu rubbed vigorously to restore circulation as we gazed at the summit now close above us.

The wind had risen, and although at first only a few mild puffs reached us it was already screaming across the summit cone, flinging a vast cloud of snow into space and ceaselessly spraying the northern rocks with freezing moisture.

At lower levels the remainder of the climb would have been absurdly easy: a short snow plug to the foot of the rocks, a steepish ascent to the final ridge, and a hundred yards of exposed rock to the top. Nevison led off, taking a step, then a rest; a step, then a rest. Time meant nothing, just the terrible strain as, muscles aching, we dragged one leg after the other.

With lungs bursting and hearts pounding we inched our way upward, now and again giving ourselves an extra-long spell as we reversed positions on the rope. At our very best we probably made little more than a hundred feet an hour while the wind increased, veered, and with a bitter, penetrating cold began to blow hard at our backs. Flurries of snow, kicked up by our boots, whirled across the ridge, writhing down the lee side in furious vortexes.

"Much wind, sahib, much wind," cried Annulu as he continued to plug away at the slope. Nevison said nothing, reserving all his energy for the last few hundred feet.

EIGHT

Disaster and Retreat

The real measure is the success or failure of the climber to triumph, not over a lifeless mountain but over himself; the true value of the enterprise lies in the example to others of human motive and human conduct.

Sir John Hunt

THE PAIN GAVE NO WARNING. It came like a giant knife, plunged into my right side, without pity and with terrible force, throwing me face down in the soft snow.

For several seconds I lay gasping in agony, fighting for breath. Each labored heave left a spray of scarlet staining the white surface, painting an all too vivid picture of ruptured blood vessels. Tom flung himself down, his face a mask of concern, but I could neither rise nor speak. For a moment I was unable to comprehend what had happened.

The realization that for me the climb had ended came quickly enough, but I could not for the moment imagine what had gone wrong. After twenty minutes or so I was able to sit up; the pain had lessened and I felt sure I would soon be able to make my way back to camp.

We were crouched not far below the windswept rock rib seen from Camp V with such high hopes just two days before. Only 350 feet to go; the thought pounded in my brain. Perhaps the others could yet make it.

I suggested to Nevison that he and Annulu leave me and complete the climb, collecting me on their return. Tom was more than dubious about the idea but suggested that we would do well to head for the shelter of the nearmost rocks, only a few hundred feet away. We could rest there and dis-

cuss the situation. In our present exposed position we were
in no way able to size up the feasibility of continuing the
climb, even if Tom should be so inclined. We could hardly
make ourselves heard above the thunderous roar of the wind
as it drove from the east, across the exposed summit ridge of
Makalu, battering the tents of our comrades in the camps below, finally hurling itself to destruction on the ramparts of
Lhotse Shar, lost to our view in the gathering cloud.

It is perhaps interesting to note that about this time the
British Nuptse expedition, in contrast to our inclement conditions, was experiencing excellent climbing weather only a
few miles to the northwest.

With Annulu keeping a firm grip on the rope in case of a
slip, Tom assisted me to my feet. A surge of pain burst
through my chest, driving me to my knees with a sob and
eliminating any possibility of my reaching the rocks. There
was no alternative. I must go down, and quickly.

I rested, lying on my side and partly doubled up, with
gloved hands clamped to my clamoring chest, unable to help
myself and hardly able to talk. We prepared to start back,
aiming for the haven of our little yellow tent, now out of
sight below us in the lee of the bergschrund.

Positions were changed on the rope. Nevison, tying a bow-
line round my waist, let me out slowly while I stumbled and
slid as far as the extended rope would allow. I lay inert, belaying as best I could, while the others worked their way
down to me. Then we began again, my crablike descent dependent largely on gravity, followed by Tom and Annulu,
carefully helping one another toward me.

I knew that we had no hope of assistance for at least two
days and in any case at that altitude it would be utterly impossible for anyone to carry or even materially help me until
we were much lower. I could depend on the others to hold
me in a fall, but other than that they were fully occupied
with getting themselves down.

I was now having difficulty with vision and for a while could not make out our ascending tracks.

In despair I tore off my snow goggles, thinking they may have clouded up or been coated with snow during one of my many falls. It was no use, I could see no better and was forced to continue down by guess or by God, swaying like a drunken pendulum, a helpless marionette at the end of twisting strings. Time and weather meant nothing. I was conscious only of the need to keep moving and of the frightening pain in my chest which allowed me to move but a few yards before resting.

I had almost completed one of my unorthodox spiderlike descents, when to my unutterable relief a blur of color from Camp VII swam into view. We worked away for another hour, until at last I found myself sitting half in half out of the tent, desperately trying to remove my crampons and get into a sleeping bag. While I lay in my bag recovering slowly, Nevison got the cooker going, looking worriedly at Annulu, who all the while just sat on his sleeping bag, strangely silent.

Gradually my condition improved and the pain began to ease, as the warmth of my bag and the hot tea had their effect. Annulu replied to questions in monosyllabic grunts that meant nothing, and Tom had still not persuaded him to drink his tea or get into his sleeping bag.

We both talked to him and after a time he managed to remove his boots and get half into his bag, promptly falling asleep, we judged by his heavy breathing. Tom saw that Annulu was as comfortable as possible, then set about getting himself bedded down.

Night had now fallen, bringing with it a lull in the wind. A few large snowflakes drifted into the partly open tent flap, settling freezingly on my face. Nevison and Annulu had done wonders in getting us safely back to camp, but I was puzzled by Annulu's uncharacteristic silence and his unwillingness to help himself, especially now, when he was relatively secure. He invariably had a ready smile, and I had found him stronger and more willing in adversity than at any other time, so I began to feel that he had been more seriously affected by altitude than I had hitherto suspected. It was not until months later that I learned he had cracked a rib during the fall above Camp VI and had said nothing about it at the time, although he was in considerable pain during the descent.

We were all three very anoxic, slow in our movements and speech and inclined to drift off into long periods of silence and drowsiness. In our brief stay above 26,000 feet Nevison and I had become thin and dehydrated, with flaccid gray faces and unkempt straggly beards. We had visibly lost weight and were a sorry sight, unable to sleep, sitting up in our bags, hands clasped around our knees trying to summon enough energy to relight our cooker.

I lay awake a good part of the night worrying unceasingly that my heart had perhaps given out and that the next day, when we would have to make the arduous descent to Camp VI, I might collapse altogether.

I knew that my comrades would never leave me alone on the mountain while I breathed, but it had now become a case of get down or perish. Later, as I leaned across Nevison to pull some gloves from my pack, a sudden resurgence of pain reminded me that it was my right side giving trouble, not my left.

Then I lay awake trying to remember if my heart was on the left or right, feeling first one side then the other to try to pin it down. Finally I concluded that it must be on the left and therefore not the cause of the trouble, when I had an awful thought: "I'm abnormal and will surely die, my heart is on the opposite side to everyone else's and is so damaged that I cannot feel it beating."

So much for the strange things anoxia will do to the mind. I am told by a medical friend that the statistical chance of dextrocardia is almost one in a million.

I do not know how long this intelligent line of reasoning continued, but I was brought fully awake by Tom crawling over my feet to look at the weather. The wind had returned, buffeting the tent with force, while in the background we could hear it roaring, faintly at first but soon with increasing velocity as it drove across the ridge above, filling the air with powdered snow and spraying a fine white coating through the tent vents onto our sleeping bags.

A terrible feeling of loneliness overcame me. I lay back, in a way almost dreading the coming of morning, when I would have to experience to an even greater extent the agony of yesterday. Disappointment and blighted hope lay like a leaden weight within me, cold comfort that we had got so high without oxygen, and even less in the forbearance of my companions, who had now to endanger their own lives in getting me down.

Gray dawn came, with little change in the wind and visibility a mere two hundred feet. I could take no food and only with difficulty managed to keep down some early-brewed tea.

Annulu seemed much better and although quiet was able to help with preparations for leaving. Tom had spent a disturbed and sleepless night, by morning looking far from well. We struggled into our clothes, helping one another where we could and taking only the absolute necessities.

Annulu helped me strap on my crampons while I prepared a light pack I intended to carry, still not fully aware of the extreme seriousness of my condition.

We were to go down in the same order as yesterday, myself first, followed by Nevison, then Annulu. I would go as far as the rope allowed, belay, then the others would join me, proceeding in a series of gigantic jerks.

I was about to start down the steep slope, when a sudden surge of nausea overwhelmed me and I vomited a small quantity of blood; every heave brought considerable pain and it was some time before I was again ready to begin the descent. I set out gingerly, sucking in all the air possible without disturbing my chest too much.

Hardly had I taken a dozen steps, however, when a wave of pain crumpled me up in the snow, one arm around my ice ax, driven through to the ice, and the other clasped to my burning side. I do not know how long I lay inert, conscious only of the frightening pain in my side and the need to keep moving down, always down. I neither knew nor cared what the others were doing; all that came through from my brain was, "Get up and take a few more steps, get up and take a few more steps."

I dumped my pack and with nothing but my ax and the life-preserving rope continued down as best I could, staggering when I was able, slithering, crawling, and sliding when I was not. Progress was painfully slow and often I must have lain mute in the snow while Nevison worked on me to get up once more and repeat the everlasting cycle toward survival and away from the easy slip into insensibility and death.

At length it became evident that at this rate we would never make Camp VI. My mind was drifting away for longer and longer periods until finally I was quite unable to get up at all.

We had dropped down only about six hundred feet and still had the difficult crossing of the glacier to contend with, a crossing of such technical difficulty that I could never hope to cope with it.

Nevison knew that the only hope of saving my life was oxygen and rest, if I could get it. Annulu volunteered to go on down alone, to send help back, and see that a tent and oxygen were sent up. He set off, doggedly determined to keep going until he reached help, while Tom turned his attention to digging out an ice cave where we could spend the night. It was now certain that we would not be able to move again before nightfall.

Digging was terribly arduous work at 26,300 feet, and before long Tom admitted that he was unable to make much progress with it, particularly as he had not been feeling well himself all day. In the meantime I had become alarmingly cold; all feeling in my feet had gone and I had spent hours trying to wiggle my toes in my heavy high-altitude boots.

By late afternoon the wind had dropped, although the sky remained very cloudy. We could see no surrounding peaks or, alas, any signs of approaching aid. We had almost given up hope of any help that night and were prepared to do the best we could without cover of any sort, a situation that would probably have meant our deaths before morning. Then, to our indescribable relief, we heard voices below us. In a matter of minutes Pember and Pasang Tenzing could be seen toiling slowly toward the steps cut by Annulu a few hours before. Never have I been so pleased to see Sherpas, and I shall not readily forget these two brave men who brought welcome salvation in the form of a tent, water, and that most sustaining of all gases, oxygen.

We were stopped only a few hundred yards from the spot where the slip occurred three days before. It was a fairly exposed position, but our two Sherpas, who seemed to have an inexhaustible supply of energy, soon had a level space cleared where Nevison had earlier attempted to dig out the ice cave.

With the tent up and a few crumbs of biscuits washed down with cold lemon drink inside me I began to feel a little better. There is no pleasure in a bivouac above 26,000 feet at any time, but this was such an improvement over the last few hours that I began to feel quite cheerful, regaining much of my lost confidence.

Pember and Pasang Tenzing started back for Camp VI, where they had left their sleeping bags, taking with them a note explaining our position and asking for oxygen. In our anoxic state earlier in the day we had neglected to give a note to Annulu, with the result that on his arrival at Camp VI he was so exhausted and excited that the others had great difficulty in getting any coherent sentences from him. He was terribly tired and dehydrated, hardly able to stand and in pain from his chest, which had given him trouble on and off all that day. (Several weeks later while I was recovering in the

United Missions Hospital in Katmandu, Annulu arrived, having walked nearly two hundred miles from the village of Khumjung. He told me that he had never expected to see me alive again and thought that both Tom and I would be found dead if ever a rescue party managed to reach us. All the time he talked he kept patting me to reassure himself, obviously thinking of the possibility that I was a ghost or at best something supernatural.)

I had not really expected to sleep much during the night, but in fact I slept better than Nevison, doubtless because of the oxygen, which I was taking at a slow flow rate. Nevison was having respiratory trouble and every now and again took a yellow tablet from a small tin of multicolored pills he carried for every conceivable situation and condition.

The next morning there was no improvement in the weather, the wind having risen once again during the night, bringing a considerable drop in temperature, which we felt through our double bags, now wet with condensation.

Unlike the French expedition of some years earlier, we were always plagued by the wind and had found to our cost that the exposed northwestern face of Makalu was no place to be caught in any sort of wind. Probably the temperature never dropped below minus 15 or 20 degrees centigrade at any time on the mountain, but this can be bitterly cold when accompanied by a wind.

Often we got hot under layers of woolen shirts, jerseys, and windproofs, but once even a moderate wind arrived, the acute oxygen shortage quickly brought us to a numbed state and we had to maintain extreme physical exertion in order to keep up any sort of normal body temperature.

Now with our damp bags and the walls of the tent covered in frost that condensed slowly, dripping water onto us much of the time, we really began to feel the cold as it seeped through us. I knew that we must have some assistance if I were to cross the icefall, as it was steep in parts and at that altitude, even with no physical handicap, technically difficult.

Our position in the frozen bivouac worsened by the hour. Because no help appeared to be forthcoming from below we determined to make a start as best we could.

In our anoxic state and under such trying conditions it is perhaps understandable that for a short while we imagined ourselves abandoned. With the passing of each minute prospects of survival seemed to slip inexorably from our grasp. With no word from our friends we foolishly supposed that they thought of us as already dead and had begun to retire down the mountain, taking the tents with them.

Needless to say, this was not so, for Ward, Harrison, and Ortenberger, aided by their Sherpas, had got the injured Ang Temba down to Camp III and were underway with a well-planned rescue attempt.

It was now May 20. Two days earlier word reached the col camp that Ang Temba and Mingma Tsering were at Camp VI and would need assistance for the remainder of the way down the mountain. Mike Ward, realizing that a sahib must get up to Camp VI as soon as possible, decided to go himself, using oxygen. Harrison and Ortenberger remained at Camp V, still planning to proceed with the next assault. However, when Ward, with Sherpa Pember Tenzing, arrived at VI, he radioed Harrison asking that all available Sherpas be sent up, as Ang Temba could now no longer walk. This automatically put "paid" to any further summit attempt. On May 19, Harrison and Ortenberger, in very unpleasant weather, had moved up to Camp VI, where they met an exhausted Ward helping the Sherpas get Ang Temba down.

Camp VI was in a miserable state; both tents had partly collapsed and the small Napper tent almost completely buried in snow. While the Sherpas prepared tea in the larger Mead tent, Harrison and Ortenberger began digging out the Napper. It was debilitating and difficult work. Harrison had vomited the night before and still felt weak. Both had their faces frosted up, and the wind chilled them to the bone.

Wind-driven drift snow blew back into the tent almost as fast as it was removed, and they still had the Mead tent to clear.

At this stage Annulu arrived, bringing the news of Nevison's and my predicament and of our request for oxygen and a tent. Harrison sent Annulu on down to Camp V while Pember and Pasang Tenzing started across the glacier carrying the Napper tent, just dug out, and the oxygen set left by Mike Ward with a thousand pounds per square inch of oxygen remaining. Harrison and Ortenberger now set about digging out the Mead tent, which was snowed up almost as badly as the Napper.

Again it was exceptionally cold, miserable work, especially as they were unable to dig properly on the side of the tent where the slope dropped steeply away and was heavily glazed with green ice.

Harrison's feet froze up and Ortenberger felt so drained that he was unable to finish and had to crawl into the tent.

They made radio contact with Romanes at Camp III, but much to their surprise heard nothing from Ward at Camp V. They were still trying to contact Mike Ward when Pember and Pasang Tenzing returned after their remarkable effort in getting the emergency equipment up to Nevison and me.

The four of them had a cold, cramped night in the tent and woke to another clear but windy day. Again they tried to contact Ward but received no reply. This was serious. They knew that they must get more support from Camp V and, most important, more oxygen.

Harrison and Ortenberger then very sensibly decided to split up, one to continue on with oxygen, a radio, and Sherpas, the other to return to Ward at Camp V for more assistance. Harrison felt strongly that he should be the one to go on, as he was fresher than Ortenberger and it was a fellow New Zealander in trouble. Finally they tossed for it, Ortenberger winning the somewhat doubtful honor of carrying on to assist us.

Harrison started back for Camp V, carrying his personal

gear and sleeping bags, wet and heavy with ice. He had a hard trip down, facing into the freezing wind, and was about done by the time he reached the tents. As he pushed his way through the doorway of the large Blanchard tent, he was confronted by a prostrate Ward, who cried in a shaky voice, "Who are you?" Harrison was staggered at first but soon realized that Ward was delirious. Without doubt his magnificent climb on Ama Dablam and the long period he had spent above 20,000 feet were taking their toll.

Meanwhile Nevison and I had almost completed preparations to leave, when Leigh Ortenberger's head appeared through the flap of the tent, much to our delight and relief. In a few seconds our sense of isolation vanished, we had once more regained touch with our comrades. Unfortunately it was now too late for me to start down. The earlier effort of preparation had given me much pain, and in my exhausted state I would have made very slow progress.

Nevison therefore decided to leave, aiming to get as low as possible while he was still able. He had felt very ill all morning, diagnosing possible pneumonia, and was greatly concerned that another night out might incapacitate him completely, giving Ortenberger the impossible task of getting us both down.

After Nevison and the Sherpas had gone, Ortenberger and I settled down to make the best of the night. I used oxygen and after a short time, with the flow rate at about two liters per minute, felt much improved, with a noticeable easing of the pain in my chest. I remember little of the night and must have slept fairly well, using the oxygen at its slowest flow rate.

The next morning I was able to keep down liquid but could eat nothing. The weather had cleared a little but was still fairly misty, with a light cold wind blowing across the glacier, making conditions unpleasant for the crossing we were about to make of the icefall.

Three of our indefatigable Sherpas, Pembertarkay, Pang-

boche Tenzing, and Siku, arrived late in the morning and after a short halt began chipping out steps across the snow
field toward the glacier. I had got into my down clothing
only with immense difficulty and assistance from Ortenberger, when I missed one of my crampons. For fully half
an hour we searched, chipping away the snow around the
tent but to my dismay it could not be found. I was now
forced to make the difficult glacier crossing with only the
one, and my heart sank at the fearful prospect.

I got the oxygen set strapped on, setting the flow rate to
four liters per minute. I immediately felt the benefit and
found myself able to stand up without too much pain, even
with the heavy weight of the oxygen equipment on my
back. We roped up and set off in single file, the Sherpas
first, clearing out the steps and doing everything they could
to help, followed by Ortenberger, then me. The Sherpas cut
and cleared steps, then, finding themselves well ahead, would
come back and help me to my feet, taking my hand whenever they could and guiding me from foothold to foothold.

Progress was lamentably slow, but I found the oxygen
making a world of difference, enabling me to take a dozen
or more steps before resting. We crossed the preliminary
snow field and had just started the difficult first stage of the
icefall when unexpectedly the single oxygen cylinder ran out.
I was left breathless and almost blacked out from the effort
of sucking nothing through the empty mask.

Ortenberger threw the cylinder away and watched it roll
down the slope and out of sight toward the Tibetan plateau
below. A Sherpa took the useless set, weighing only a few
pounds now, and left me once again with only my ice ax to
carry.

We moved on over the glacier, but I was having such
difficulty that night fell before we were within sight of
Camp VI.

How I managed to remain on that steep face of the glacier
I do not know. Often the boot without a crampon slipped

from its hold, threatening to precipitate me down the slope and possibly tear Ortenberger from his insecure belay. At eight o'clock that evening we reached the single tent of Camp VI.

It was windless and bitterly cold. We were all exhausted and my right hand was badly frostbitten from contact with the steel head of the ice ax. I had worn double gloves until the icefall was reached, but with one crampon missing I had to take more weight on the hands to maintain my balance. For this reason I had been forced to remove a glove in order to retain a good grip on ax and rope.

Urkein had waited at Camp VI for our arrival and was keeping hot tea ready, but we took so much longer than expected that he ran out of fuel. By the time we arrived the tea was as frozen as ourselves.

We all huddled together to begin the longest night of our lives, with nothing to drink and unable to eat. With but three sleeping bags among the five of us our plight was unenviable.

Leigh Ortenberger gave one of his down sleeping bags to a Sherpa and his down pants to another, while Urkein had my down jacket. I could feel nothing and was only partly sensible of what was going on, even though I was using oxygen for sleeping. A partly consumed bottle was at this camp with about three-quarters remaining; this I used on and off during the night and the little that was left during the next day.

Urkein spent some time trying to restore circulation to my frozen hand, but with little success. He finally held it over the flame of a candle and, as I could feel nothing, held it so close that by the time I realized that the delicious aroma was me the skin on two fingers was hanging in burned shreds.

The night was one long, endless, numb horror, relieved by short periods of sleep using the oxygen. Dawn at last came and with it more wind. I was barely conscious of getting away and made heavy work of it. Even with the oxygen I was so weak that the weight of the equipment probably negated the usefulness of the gas. Every few steps I collapsed and forced myself to my feet only after a rest and a gasp. At times I lay in the snow unable to move, gasping with the pain in my chest and almost smothered, the weight of the oxygen set on my back, pressing my face down into the snow.

After an hour or so the supply ran out. I was almost pleased to see the empty bottle roll away to oblivion, not that the reduction in weight seemed to help at all. The way was still so steep that I could not be carried and could be assisted only from the front or behind. Time after time I fell, lying inert until Ortenberger, coiling the rope as he came, shook me and talked me back into reality. With consciousness returned I could barely summon the strength to take a few more faltering steps before again collapsing.

After five days above 26,000 feet and four days of severe pain, dehydration, and exhaustion, my mind began to wander. I had a fixation to keep moving and was continually conscious of the need to force myself to my feet whenever I collapsed. However, I now began to have periods when I left the mountain and thought I was back in New Zealand. Several times I found myself on the beach near my home; my wife and children were playing in the water and I was always in the same place, lying on the sand near the beach. I desperately wanted to go down to the water myself, but the sand was so warm I kept drifting off to sleep and did not seem able either to get up or to call out to them.

When these hallucinations occurred, Ortenberger had great difficulty in kicking me back to sensibility; at times I resented his interference with my sleep on the beach and tried to ignore him. I have no doubt that his patience and perseverance plus his determination to keep me moving, however much pain I was in, saved my life and I acknowledge my debt to him.

I became obsessed with thirst and remember talking to Leigh about California oranges and inquiring rather petulantly why he did not give me one.

Later in the day Sherpas arrived from Camp V, sent up by John Harrison to help us in. Knowing of my fondness for lemon tea, Harrison had thoughtfully given them a water bottle full for me. I managed to get a few swallows, and then, not realizing how damaged my hand was, dropped the container and lost the remainder.

At length we reached a place where the surface leveled out, angling moderately toward the steep edge of the Makalu Col. From here the Sherpas were able to carry me, taking turns of ten minutes or so each, with me sitting on their backs in the loop of a long headband, in much the way they carried a normal load.

I remember little of the remainder of the journey except that it got dark and very cold.

But there is one thing I shall never forget; hearing Urkein and his Sherpa friends competing with one another for turns at carrying me. We were still above 25,000 feet, a height where a man needed every ounce of breath and energy for himself, but this loyalty and keenness to help those stricken on a mountain are typical of the Sherpa people. Many a Sherpa has lost his life, when he might have got safely down, through remaining behind to help an injured climber.

In the darkness there was some difficulty in locating Camp V, but at long last we arrived and I fell gratefully into the hands of my friends, who had hot tea, warm sleeping bags, and morphine ready. The end had come to the longest and most painful day of my life, and although I did not know it then, the last day I would ever walk on my own two legs.

NINE

"Pinished"

He wakes, who never thought to wake again,
who held the end was death.

Rupert Brooke

"NEVER HAVE I SEEN ANYONE nearer to being a corpse than
Peter—his eyes were sunken and lifeless, his breath came in
uneven shudders and his colour was dreadful. Nevertheless,
there was life and he was now in our hands." So wrote John
Harrison a few hours after my belated arrival in Camp V.

It is impossible to describe the heartfelt joy and the wave
of relief that overwhelmed me as I was delivered into the
hands of my friends and countrymen. No longer did my
destiny depend on a tired Leigh Ortenberger, the exhausted,
loyal, and courageous band of Sherpas, and my own efforts,
which had been pushed to the extremes of endurance. I knew
that I was saved and I was profoundly thankful for it.

True, I looked like death, and with good reason Harrison
was appalled by my awful appearance. He was not to know
then how this providential return to the bosom of my friends
had gladdened my heart and refreshed my will to survive.
Common danger and common hardship mold the perfect
mountain friendship. In times of danger and difficulty on a
mountain a man taps unsuspected reservoirs of spiritual
strength, both in himself and in his friends. Together they
respond instinctively to the call of comradeship and to the
common bond of experience, forged on a great mountain,
such as Makalu. Fortunate indeed is the man who has placed

his faith, and his life, in the hands of his friends and found them not wanting.

What temptations and agonies of indecision Harrison and West must have suffered on that longest of days, May 22, 1961. What was happening above them they knew not. They were sure that everything possible that could be done for the rescued and rescuers had been done. Nonetheless they were plagued by fears, for they could see little of the wind-swept peak above, and reassuring glimpses of the returning climbers were denied them.

As the day wore on their doubts increased. Should they go out and help their exhausted comrades? What help could they give without oxygen? All they would succeed in doing, were they to climb higher, would be to exhaust themselves; who would there be then fit enough to take the injured men over the col to Camp III. The situation was not one that called for misplaced heroics, but rather for clear thinking and an appreciation of the over-all problems involved.

To climb can be defined as to go up or to go down. Mountaineering, however, is nothing quite as simple. It is a compendium of hard-won knowledge, of regard for the elements, and an understanding of environment. It is an awakening of experience, sometimes scarcely noticed, at other times eagerly sought and absorbed, in the manner of a sponge. The mountaineer must know the weather and its vagaries, he must read the snows and heed the imperceptible changes that transform the safe slope into one of danger. He must have health, endurance, aptitude, and agility. He will be the better man if he has imagination and perhaps a sense of humor, but above all, in difficult situations he must make decisions, and they must invariably be right.

Harrison and West had known that they must remain at Camp V. They arranged for more oxygen to be brought up and they discussed the situation by radio with Romanes at Camp III. Romanes prepared his tired Sherpas to start back to the Makalu Col early next morning. As it grew dark Harrison and West had cooked food, melted snow for water, and warmed up sleeping bags. As well they had, for we were completely frosted up on arrival and were desperately grateful for the warm, dry sleeping bags. We were received with compassion and kindness by those on the col, Sherpa and sahib alike. Warmth and hot tea were ready and before long I began to feel better.

I remember little of the night, except that I was unable to bring any feeling back into my feet and that the condition of my hands worried me a good deal.

In the morning I awoke before dawn and knew by the rhythmic flapping of the tent that the wind still blew. The smallest movement hurt my chest, forcing me to cough and throw up small quantities of blood. I certainly did not feel good, but I hoped that the warmth and rest might bolster my strength for the next stage. John West decided that I should not attempt to move until the oxygen arrived, as I was quite unable to walk without it. Leigh Ortenberger, who was a bit the worse for wear after his efforts of the past few days, decided to start down the mountain, taking four tired Sherpas with him. They could be of little help to us and every extra day they remained made it more difficult for them to make the return journey safely.

Just before five in the afternoon we heard Sherpa voices through a lull in the wind. Shortly Purchita's grinning face appeared, followed by Phurkepa and Nima Namgyal, carrying oxygen bottles. It was too late for the start down, so everyone resigned himself to another night above 24,000 feet. For my part I was past caring and only partly conscious of the passage of time. I had the foolish notion that a few more days' rest on the col would do me good and that I would soon be strong again. The reverse, of course, was the case, and although John West said nothing, he was becoming increasingly worried. Harrison had spent much of the day working on our malfunctioning gas cookers. After a long struggle he got them going satisfactorily and in celebration heated up a tin of grapefruit juice, left by the French expedition of 1955. I remember having a few sips and thinking it delicious.

The following morning we heard by radio that Romanes with a strong party of Sherpas had left Camp III. He was using oxygen, so he expected to make good time.

I was very much afraid of being moved, as the slightest effort caused my chest to pain damnably. In addition I still had the fixation that all I needed was a little more rest, and resolutely opposed suggestions that I put on my crampons.

West, however, was firm, and by 10 A.M. I found myself dressed and the unwilling wearer of a twenty-four pound oxygen set. With West and Harrison supporting me on either side, I staggered a few yards, but my legs simply refused to keep going and I collapsed, bringing the others down with me. We tried again, this time dispensing with the heavy oxygen set, but it was no use.

Harrison, who knew that I must be taken down that day or never, tried to persuade me to let him piggyback me. This I had enough sense to refuse resolutely, as, apart from killing me, it would almost certainly have killed him also. He could never have hoped to get safely over the steep and exposed edge of the col with a dead weight on his back. These attempts at walking had again left me in considerable pain, and West decided to give me morphine. Harrison, who realized that a new approach must be made, tackled the problem with that sense of improvisation and ingenuity with which many New Zealanders imagine they are born. He collected three "mountain mule" pack frames plus twelve middle sections of Mead tent poles and plenty of rope. These he lashed into a rickety stretcher-come-sledge under the eyes of the contemptuous Sherpas, who were all feeling the cold and thought Harrison Sahib was just wasting time.

Meanwhile I was explaining to John West a long, involved plan I had for remaining on the col while everyone else left.

I would gather strength and come on down in a few days. West was very polite and agreed with all I said. He explained my plan in detail to Wally Romanes, who had just arrived, and together they lashed me, sleeping bags and all, to Harrison's sledge. The next thing I remember is waking up in Camp III, almost five thousand feet lower down the mountain. It was as well for me that I was unconscious, for had I been aware of the perilous situations on the way down I would certainly have died of fright. The fixed ropes were a tremendous help, as in many places the sledge was simply clipped to them with a karabiner and slid along in perfect security. On the steep pitches the sledge was inched along while Romanes retained control by guidelines and with secure belays.

By 5:30 P.M. they reached Camp IV and despite the lateness of the hour decided to press on down to Camp III. I was completely unconscious and every so often West checked my pulse to make sure I was still alive.

Fortunately the wind had lessened, though it was bitterly cold all the way, and everyone worked with a will. Down the steep couloir and across the diagonal ice traverse they went, using the fixed rope. Soon darkness fell across the great "schrund" toward Camp III, now visible less than a half hour away.

It was "plain sailing" now for the Sherpas, who forged ahead, towing the sledge behind them. Now that the crisis was over, Romanes and Harrison, who was having trouble with frostbitten feet, fell behind, and they arrived at camp in almost total darkness. Everyone was absolutely finished and beaten except me, whose life had just been saved. To the late arrivals I appeared nauseatingly healthy, to judge by Harrison's diary once more: "By the time Wally and I reached the tents, the now awake Peter was already installed, with a mug of his favourite lemon tea in his hand and looking surprisingly none the worse for his rough trip."

The change in altitude had certainly worked wonders. I

not only felt much better but was able to think clearly once more and for the first time in weeks, it seemed, I fell into a dreamless sleep.

Mike Gill, Tom Nevison, and Mike Ward had already moved on down to Camp II. Ward was slowly improving after his experience on the col at Camp V, but he was still far from well. In some ways his reactions on the col were similar to mine. He had not realized how ill he was and had steadfastly refused to start down the col, even in the face of John West's insistence. West, breathing fire and efficiency, had returned to Camp V, bringing more oxygen and a fresh batch of Sherpas. He quickly realized that Ward, in his delirious state, must go down as soon as possible and after much persuasion finally bundled him over the col in company with Nevison and some Sherpas.

Using oxygen, Nevison reached Camp IV in an hour and a half, but Ward, also using oxygen, had deteriorated so badly that he took five hours to complete the same journey, and then he only just made it.

I think we all awoke with an immense feeling of relief at being away from the wind of the col. After so many days of being torn at and buffeted it seemed strange and unreal to live in a perfectly still tent where one could converse without having to shout. John Harrison, whose frost-bitten feet were troubling him, set out early for Camp I. I was sledged down the glacier by John West and Wally Romanes, assisted by a large group of Sherpas.

They were all very pleased at being almost off the mountain, and they talked and chattered away as they manhandled the sledge over the rough patches.

On May 27 we arrived at Camp I. I had experienced an unpleasant time negotiating the glacier between Camps II and I. Mike Gill, assisted by a strong group of Sherpas headed by Urkein, took over bringing me down from Camp II. Unfortunately, with the rough and steep moraine walls where the Makalu Glacier meets the Barun, it was impossible to use

the sledge. On the way down I developed a terrible thirst
and at every stop threatened to extinguish Mike Gill's good
humor with my constant requests for water. Short of light-
ing a fire to melt snow he had no way of collecting it.
Fortunately for me, one of the Sherpas found a few trickles
of slowly thawing ice which he painstakingly collected in
a water bottle. As a measure of the severity of our dehydration, I was interested to observe that, although I greedily
soaked up all the water I could get, it was only once, and
that to my undying shame, that I needed to urinate during
the several days elapsing between Camp V and our arrival
in Katmandu.

Urkein and his friends once again stepped into the breach
and I was piggybacked like a sack of coal. The strain of a
long day's jolting started my chest trouble again, and I was
almost unconscious when we at last reached Camp I.

From there we were in radio contact with the Silver Hut,
where Desmond Doig used our powerful short-wave transmitter to summon help. The Americans, who controlled the
high-performance Bell helicopter, immediately made it available and we received word that we could expect it on
May 29.

It was clearly impossible for a helicopter to land at Camp
I, which was located in the midst of pile upon pile of glacial
boulders. In any case our camp at 17,000 feet was above the
safe landing height for this aircraft.

Once again I had to be carried, sitting in a Sherpa's headband. They took turns bearing my dead weight on their backs,
and after four hours we reached a suitable site for a helicopter
landing. Here at 15,000 feet we pitched camp and hoped that
the weather would remain fine for the morrow's flight. The
rough trip down the glacier had further aggravated my
chest and I experienced a very unpleasant night. Several times
I coughed blood until finally John West gave me some tablets
and I was able to sleep.

In the morning the Sherpas gathered what little wood they

could find and lit a smoky fire as a guide for the pilot. We were surrounded by high peaks and the only possible entrance for an aircraft was over a snow-covered saddle just visible some miles down the valley. The morning wore on and we became more and more anxious. With the fast-approaching monsoon we could not expect a full day's clear weather, and we knew that the helicopter must get inland and return before midday.

Snow-threatening gray clouds streamed across the great peaks near the head of the Barun as, almost without warning, the helicopter appeared above the camp and was quickly lost to view still heading up valley. How insignificant an aircraft could look, dwarfed by the enormity of the mountains around it. Even the familiar clatter of the rotor blades was dulled by the millions of tons of gray-green ice and glacier debris sprawled across the valley floor.

Catching sight of the colored tents of Camp I, the pilot, flying low, soon realized that we were farther down valley and turned about. To our relief we saw him note our smoke and head toward us. As there were four of us to go out— Mike Ward, John West, Ang Temba, with a damaged ankle, and myself—the pilot decided to make his rescue in four flights; the first stage was to the Nepalese village of Num, near the Arun River, only a half hour downstream.

Here Ward and I would wait while the pilot flew back and picked up Ang Temba and John West. Then he would do one flight of three hours to Katmandu with Ward and me, returning the following day for the other two.

With some difficulty I was moved into a sitting position alongside the pilot with Mike Ward beside me. We waved good-by to the others while the motor was revved to full power. Nothing happened. The aircraft refused to lift and no amount of coaxing seemed to make the slightest difference. In the rarefied atmosphere the machine was operating at the limits of its capability, and it began to look as though Ward would have to get out. The pilot made several adjust-

ments to the pitch of the rotor blades by alternately watching his instruments, switching off, and clambering out to attack the heavy blades with a large wrench. To our intense
relief, after twenty minutes of trial and error, we lifted
shakily over the glacier and flew slowly toward the pass.

At first we flew only a few hundred feet above the valley
floor, the mountains towering on either side about us. We
were soon into the Barun gorge, still hemmed in by peaks,
which rapidly closed around us as we soared down valley
toward the wide Arun River. To our left a short rocky
promontory pushed into the river. Behind it lay a small clearing beside a tumbling mountain stream that burst from the
heavy bush to meet the Arun in a welter of foam and flying
spray.

On a cleared ridge a short distance from the stream stood
the small, isolated Nepalese village of Num. The villagers,
scattered among the houses, gazed in astonishment as we
swept in to land. The pilot expertly dropped into the deserted
clearing beside the stream and, helped by Mike Ward, lifted
me out. Just as I was made comfortable by the banks of the
stream, the whole population of the village arrived, to watch
in amazement as the helicopter circled above them. The pilot
wasted no time in returning to collect West and Ang Temba,
as the grim Barun gorge was slowly beginning to fill with
clouds. Mike Ward went down the short, scrub-covered track
to the river, where he sat soaking his feet amid an interested
audience of Nepalese washerwomen.

As usual I seemed to be racked with thirst, which wasn't
helped by my inability to move out of the strong sun. I lay
in the open on an old sleeping bag, the center of an admiring
throng of village elders and chubby-faced children. I understood little of their remarks, but the general meaning was
quite clear.

"The sahibs have been driven from the mountain by the
wrath of the gods and the sahib's bird is afraid and has flown

away. Both the sahibs are sick, but the old one with the beard who lies on the ground is very sick."

By this time the old one was becoming increasingly distressed by the hot sun. A kindly Nepalese woman came forward and held a wide-leafed branch over my head, shading my face. Following her example, the other villagers collected a pile of branches and built a shade fence around me. I was profoundly touched and tried to indicate this as best I could by smiling and waving my hand.

I asked for water in Hindustani, saying, *"Panee lao,"* and pointing to my mouth. I was understood immediately and a young boy was quickly dispatched to the river for a dish of water. It was ice cold and I lay back luxuriously enjoying the liquid coolness and the feel of green grass and trees after so many months away from them.

I had lain dozing for some time when there arose a commotion among the watchers and an authoritative-looking Nepali stepped into view. He fixed me with a commanding stare and an overwhelming odor of garlic. As he came toward me I noted that the soles of his feet were thick and plated like the shell of an armadillo. Rifts and fissures ran through them where the skin had split and healed, like sunbaked clay, and horny calluses showed across the ball of each toe, like a string of well-placed football cleats. He had a sharp, foxlike face with slanting black eyes beneath a cloth hat that was secured to his stringy hair by a large wooden skewer. His robe was plum red and shapeless, a mixture of Nepali design and Tibetan colors. He was clearly the village medicine man or witch doctor and as such commanded great respect.

He looked me up and down and then, bending low, felt me all over with both his hands. Seemingly not satisfied with my uninspiring shape, he produced a small colored bag from around his neck and placed it upon my forehead. Overcome by this unlooked-for attention, I lay there, endeavoring to balance the musty-smelling bag on the bridge of my nose and at the same time appear as appreciative as possible. He turned, and began to harangue the onlookers, whose attention had begun to shift from his extraordinary performance to the helicopter, as it came into sight downriver.

John West arrived with Ang Temba, and I immediately pressed our Sherpa, who understood the dialect, to tell me what the medicine man was saying. They exhanged a few words, and again I asked for a translation. Everyone began to talk at once, and Ang Temba, who had at first conversed effusively, suddenly dried up, claiming that he was unable to remember this particular dialect. Not unnaturally I grew suspicious and at the risk of knocking the witch doctor's bag from my brow, insisted on an explanation. Ang Temba looked intensely uncomfortable, and just as he was about to speak the witch doctor, silencing him with a commanding glare, turned toward me and in almost faultless English said succinctly, "Sahib pinished."

With that he collected his bag and departed, doubtless well satisfied with his day's work. To say that he made an impression on me, and a gloomy one at that, is to put it mildly. I soon recovered, however, as I reckoned that it would take more than the inside of a camel's stomach, or whatever it was that he had in the bag, to finish me off.

John West and Ang Temba prepared to spend the night at Num, where the villagers treated them with great kindness. Ward and I set off once more in the helicopter for Katmandu, over three hours' flying away.

The clouds were now thick and it was some time before we were able to find the right route through the mountains. We edged our way down deep valleys and around heavily wooded spurs. At times we thought we might have to turn back, for the flight had become decidedly difficult. The pilot had no time to talk; he was concentrating on his navigation and in dodging the heavy cloud formations. With superb flying skill he edged the helicopter over the last pass and we broke out of the cloud into the clear skies of the Katmandu Valley.

Sick and battered though I felt after the terrible struggle for survival on Makalu, it was as though a great adventure, rather than a misadventure, had at last ended. In reality it was but the beginning.

TEN

Shanta Bhawan

"As the dew is dried up by the morning sun, so are the sins of man by the sight of Himachal, In a thousand ages of the Gods I could not tell thee of the glories of Himachal."

Hindu saying

FOR MANY YEARS Nepal was a completely closed land, remaining aloof at official levels to the feelings of the people and the influence of foreign cultures alike. Indeed the country was virtually run by and for one large and supremely influential family, the Rana. So much so that its last hundred years of history came to be characterized by "Ranarchy," from the family name of its autocratic rulers.

A fast-moving series of events brought about the revolution of 1950, which reinstated King Mahendra Bikram Shah to the throne of the ancient Himalayan kingdom. The country was opened to foreigners interested in improving and developing the land, and a constitutional democratic rule was established.

Ambitious plans affecting natural resources, health services, education, and local government were implemented, based largely on foreign aid. Technicians and advisers as well as money and tools poured into the country from Russia, the United States, China, India, and other interested parties. The old Nepali culture began to stir, forced by these large-scale developmental changes to adapt itself to the inevitable urge to keep abreast of the modern world.

As a result of a direct invitation from the Ministry of Health of His Majesty's Government, a medical aid program was instituted under the auspices of the United Mission to Nepal. This ecumenical Christian organization was given one of the old Rana palaces at Shanta Bhawan, just outside Katmandu, to house the first reasonably modern hospital in Nepal. It was in a sun-baked, dusty, plowed field alongside this hospital that the helicopter now landed.

A sea of curious Nepali faces watched as I was lifted carefully onto a stretcher carried by two Indian medical orderlies. Jimmy Dick, the Scottish doctor who was to look after me for the remainder of my time in Katmandu, began a quick examination before allowing the stretcher to be moved the hundred yards or so to the hospital building. As he peeled off my gloves, a murmur ran through the curious but sympathetic crowd. The right hand was badly swollen, the index finger and thumb already turning black, while the remainder of the hand had a peculiar putty-like consistency, as though it had been filled to the bursting point with water. The left hand showed little swelling, but each knuckle was capped with a black layer of dead tissue and was bleeding in places where the effort of supporting myself in the helicopter had parted the blistered skin.

I had no feeling whatever in my feet, which were still encased in eider-down boots. Happily, for the present, the pain in my chest had mercifully eased.

I was very hot and apart from my preoccupation with a raging thirst could not understand why this should be so. I had quite forgotten that I was still dressed for 27,000 feet and we were now down to a little over 4000 feet on a warm day.

I croaked for water, with a sudden vehemence that startled myself almost as much as the crowd, some of whom imagined me already dead. There was probably every reason for this assumption, as, emaciated as I was by dehydration, I must have made a pitiable sight. Poorly bearded below a face blistered by both sun and frostbite, the whole could only have resembled the deathly gray pallor of an Assyrian wall painting.

Guessing that I was probably dehydrated and in need of liquid, a Nepalese member of the hospital staff produced the major representative of the local lemonade sellers' union. This grubby, unkempt individual pressed forward, clutching a large, suspiciously murky-looking bottle, the label outrageously proclaiming the contents as related to a well-known brand of gin. In my advanced state of thirst Gunga Din himself could not have been more welcome, nor received with greater cordiality. With a grateful gurgle I drained the contents, oblivious of the interesting possibilities of its origin. Came it direct from the sacred waters of the Bhagmati or brewed from a paddy-field puddle I knew not, nor did I care; it was wet and my very soul craved for it.

In fact it proved to be a particularly sweet and biliously colored product of what the Nepalese fondly imagined was "American type" Coca-Cola. Nonetheless I have the memory of that thirst-quenching draught with me still, while other supposedly thirsty days are now long since forgotten.

The hospital porters carried my stretcher through the stone-flagged ground floor of the two-story building. A curiously out-of-place marble staircase, a relic of more flamboyant days, curved toward my room. The porters, living examples of the long and short of it, insisted on transporting the stretcher on their heads, the tall one, for some incomprehensible reason, in the lead. Going up the stairs produced a moment of tension when at an alarming angle I was almost precipitated headfirst into the ornate lobby below, in the manner of the central figure at a burial at sea.

I was put to bed in a small, freshly painted room, the double window overlooking the old palace garden, with the hospital guesthouse in the courtyard, directly below. Miss Fleming, a kindly, middle-aged Irish nursing sister, took charge and peremptorily ordered me washed.

This gargantuan project took considerably longer than expected, as I had first to be carefully extricated from a multifarious collection of much-worn jerseys, shirts, and down clothing. My feet were uncovered for the first time in many days and gave terrifying evidence of the nightmare retreat from Makalu. They were swollen from above the ankle to almost twice normal size. The toes and soles were already brick hard to the touch, while the heels were a sinister brown and violet color—the whole without feeling. I was horror-struck by their awful appearance and eagerly sought reassurance from Dr. Dick.

"My God, what shall I do, how much can be saved?"

"It looks pretty grim, I admit," said Jimmy Dick ruefully, "but it is far too early to tell yet, and besides they probably look much worse than they really are."

Little mollified, I lay like a freshly emerged chrysalis, barely conscious of Sister Fleming busily scraping me clean. With the removal of three months' accumulated grime and the cleaning away of sundry burned skin around my fingers, I was returned to an almost human color and began to feel a little better.

The drop in altitude had greatly eased my breathing, and I now found that the pain in my chest troubled me only when I attempted to move or inadvertently breathed deeply. Jimmy Dick diagnosed the trouble in my lung as primary pulmonary thrombosis with infarction, and he was amazed that I had survived the first onslaught, much less the terrible descent to Camp V.

"You must realize, Peter," he said, "you have been saved by an absolute miracle. Normally, pulmonary thrombosis at almost 28,000 feet would mean sudden death, and you can thank God that you are here at all. It is important that you get to a modern hospital, preferably in New Zealand, as soon as possible, so that your frostbite can be properly treated. Our aim at Shanta Bhawan will be to get you well enough to travel, so that at the very earliest you may get the best treatment available."

This suited me, as I was naturally anxious to get home as soon as possible, although I was privately and quixotically determined not to leave Katmandu until I could walk. I had no wish to arrive back in New Zealand on a stretcher. I would probably be on my feet again in a few weeks. I still did not realize how serious the frostbite was. For that matter, neither did Jimmy Dick.

He had never seen frostbite before and was unfamiliar with its treatment, although he kept this from me initially. He certainly understood the pathology of the problem well enough, but had not had the chance to practice the thera-peutics. His first thought was an attempt at restoring circula-tion to the extremities with a series of spinal injections, designed to open the arteries and improve blood flow. He promised "a stab at this," as he put it, for first thing the fol-lowing morning.

(For notes on the medical aspects of the expedition, the reader is referred to the Appendix for extracts from a paper by Michael Ward.)

It was now the end of May, the middle of the hot season in Katmandu, with the day temperatures rising toward eighty degrees Fahrenheit. I was thankful to be covered only by a sheet, although Jimmy Dick insisted on my keeping both feet exposed to the air, as he was informed that frostbite should be kept cool and if possible in free-circulating air.

At first I was distressed at the unwelcome prospect of lying in bed continually faced with the vivid reminders of the past few weeks, and, worse, with the dread possibilities of the future. How much of each foot could be saved? Would I ever climb again? What would be the reaction of the New Zealand Navy if I lost all my toes; would I be medically discharged from the service? What, then, of my family, how could I support them? These and a hundred other thoughts surged through my brain as I lay contemplating the offend-ing members of my extremities. As the days passed the dark areas around each sole extended, until both feet became quite black almost to the ankle and I gradually but irrevocably lost the ability to move any of my toes.

This business of keeping my feet exposed led to an incident that in retrospect I found amusing, but at the time afforded me little enough pleasure. I lay in bed one day in a state of semitorpor, drifting intermittently off to sleep as a pain-killing injection took effect. Gradually I became aware of several people standing in a semicircle around my bed, observing me with a more than casual interest. A voice whose owner could only have come from the Deep South of the United States remarked that perhaps I had better not be touched, as maybe I was "just a mite sick."

This masterly understatement struck me as particularly unintelligent and succeeded in making me feel like some strange but interesting zoological exhibit. They were, I later found, a party of American tourists on a twelve-day round-the-world tour. Having apparently seen all there was to be seen in Katmandu during their half-day visit, they were viewing the hospital before catching the plane for Calcutta. By some mischance they had accidentally found their way unescorted into my room. It was clear that they had no idea what had befallen me or who, or for that matter what, I was. One bespectacled elderly lady, heedless of her colleagues' instruction not to touch, persistently tapped the end of my exposed blackened big toe with her pencil, a process that hardly endeared her to me.

They had just left, happily, when one of their number abruptly returned. He waved a large multilensed movie camera under my nose and thoughtfully requested that he might take some movies. I declined with some heat, whereupon he rather surprisingly raised his hat, shook me warmly by the wrist, remarked that he had met my type before, and as abruptly departed.

This observation left me somewhat confused, and I could only presume that he imagined I had been captured in a re-

mote part of Nepal and was some sort of black-footed specimen of whatever I was supposed to be.

With the help of sedatives I slept most of the first night
at Shanta Bhawan, but my mind was still tormented with the
terrors of the descent from Makalu. I tossed and turned,
sometimes crying out, so that the little Nepali nurse sitting
by my bedside became afraid and sent for Jimmy Dick.

The next morning I awoke, too weak to sit up without
help and unable to keep down any food. I still had a raging
thirst and was encouraged to drink as much as possible.

I craved the lemonade type of soft drink, but in Nepal
anything drinkable of that sort was practically unobtainable
except to Americans, who had the use of a well-stocked
commissary provided by their Aid Organization. Fortunately,
during the whole of my stay at Shanta Bhawan, I had as
much fruit juice and soft drink as I needed through the generosity of some American friends.

The expedition, of course, had earlier made many friends
in Katmandu, and principal among them were the executives
of an American firm that was installing communication equipment throughout Nepal under the American Point Four
Program. These families, Ralph and Marge Dennis, Ralph and
Joyce Beacon, and Sam and Geneva Mazza, gave us the run
of their homes in the typical openhearted American way and
had assisted the expedition with communication and helicopter transport problems. It seemed strange to us New Zealanders, used to comparatively frugal morning fare and rarely
visiting friends before midday, to be invited to the Beacons'
for early breakfast. We would be plied with ham and eggs
and coffee, followed by pancakes with copious quantities of
maple syrup, until we could eat no more and were pleased
to take our protesting digestive systems off to the Solu
Khumbu. Here our meals were seasoned with the good sauce
of hunger and we were always ready for anything the Sherpa
cooks offered us.

While I was in hospital in Katmandu, my American friends

kept me supplied with tinned lime and soda, imported from the United States. As I got through about six cans a day, I hate to think what it must have cost them. For several nights after my arrival in Shanta Bhawan, Marge Dennis and Joyce Beacon, both of whom were trained nurses, took it in turns to sit by my bed. Often I would awake to see one of them dozing in the hard chair by the window, the ampoules and needles on a little tray ready for my regular two-hourly injection. These injections never worried me; they were invariably given in the upper arm and I rarely felt them.

The spinal injections, however, were a different thing altogether. Not that they hurt much of themselves. Jimmy Dick usually put a little local anesthetic into the area where he wished to make the injection, and all I felt was an unpleasant pushing sensation in the small of the back. It was the aftermath of the first injection that worried me. This dilated the arteries and set the blood flowing back through the tortured tissue of both feet. At first I felt a warm glow flooding through my lower limbs to my feet. My legs seemed to pulse with life once more and by a concentration of effort I was able to wiggle the big toes very slightly. In less than two hours the warmth had disappeared. The old helpless leaden feeling returned and with it came the most appalling pain. As though the needle had unlocked a hidden well of torment, my feet burst into a searing fire of agonized throbbing. My body writhed as my determination to do without analgesics withered and my mind so filled with pain that I was given an injection of pethidine and merciful sleep.

Thus began the gradual infiltration of that invidious drug throughout my nervous system, accompanied by the relentless sapping of my will power. In the months to come my dependence on the drug became so great that I was unable to differentiate between pain and the need for pethidine.

It was unfortunate at the outset that so much analgesic was needed, but although Jimmy Dick changed the drug as often as possible, using various morphine derivatives and certain synthetics, the average pethidine dosage worked out at a hundred milligrams every two hours.

I awoke in a lather of sweat, with the sheets and pillow-case soaking and great beads of perspiration clouding my brow. I assumed that the excessive sweating was something to do with the injection, for although the room was humid the altitude of Katmandu cooled the air, making the day warm and pleasantly drowsy, reminiscent of a summer's day in New Zealand.

Long streamers of dark cloud, the advancing portents of an early monsoon, scudded briskly toward the distant mountains, filling the valleys with gray mist and showering the naked tops with fresh snow. To the mountaineer this comes as a warning. To the countless thousands living by the great rivers snaking across the Indian plains below it should have come as an ominous sign, but all too often it went unheeded. Even now, as from time immemorial, the first trickles of melted snow had begun to swell the river headwaters. Soon the rising tide would sweep away the flimsy bridges across the Dudh Kosi and the Arun, driving on for hundreds of miles to catch Indian villages up in the fierce onslaught of floodwaters, cast upon the plains by the uncontrolled Himalayan watersheds.

Jimmy Dick stood by the bed, his battered stethoscope dangled loosely from his jacket pocket. His instruments lay in disorderly array in an open child's school case on a nearby chair.

"Now, about those toes," he said, "can you wiggle them?" I tried, but absolutely nothing happened. They remained immovable, no matter how much effort of mind and muscle I put into them.

"It's hopeless," I said in despair. "There's nothing can be done. I shall have to have them all off."

"That may be so," said Jimmy thoughtfully, "but the spinal injections will certainly help and there is no knowing how much tissue may recover in time."

This was true, but there was little satisfaction in knowing it, for in my heart I guessed that there was now no hope for my toes. My thoughts turned to Maurice Herzog, the courageous Frenchman who lost his fingers and toes during the successful French ascent of Annapurna. What one can do another can, I thought. Why, he even climbed the Matterhorn after three years in hospital; so surely I could do as well.

These thoughts were a help, but at the same time I began to realize that I was not going to be able to walk before returning to New Zealand and would probably travel as a stretcher case.

The night grew dark. Father Marshall Moran, ghostly in his long white cassock, slipped into the room and sat by my bed. I drifted into wakefulness and was about to switch on the light, when he stopped my hand with a chuckle, saying, "Don't turn on that light, you don't want me to be caught with a Protestant, do you?" I laughed, pleased at a little comic relief.

"Seriously," he said, "you are not supposed to have visitors, but I just wanted you to know that I have spoken to Ed Hillary by radio at Khumjung, and he tells you to be of good cheer, he is on his way out as fast as possible, and should see you in little more than a week."

I was delighted to hear news of Ed and to learn that the school was now complete at Khumjung, with Tem Dorje, the Sherpa schoolmaster, already taking his first class.

The days passed, and although I still could not sit up easily I began to take more food and to need less liquid. Every morning Sister Fleming produced fresh fruit, eggs, milk, or some such delicacy for breakfast, anxious to get me strong enough for a small operation Jimmy Dick wanted to perform on my right hand.

Where the hand had been burned by Urkein's overenthusiastic ministrations the flesh was raw, and on the underside of the two middle fingers a split skin graft was needed. The fresh skin would be taken from the upper arm, where the scars would be fairly inconspicuous.

I was taken to the ground floor, where Jimmy Dick and Betty Milledge, who was to administer the anesthetic, waited in the hospital's modestly equipped operating theater. Jim Milledge's wife, Betty, herself a doctor, was voluntarily working at Shanta Bhawan while she waited for her husband's return with Hillary. (The Milledges later gave up excellent prospects in England to work at the Christian Medical College in Southern India.)

In the theater, as he prepared for the operation, Jimmy told me of a complex skin graft he had performed on a young Nepali huntsman a few days earlier. A large Himalayan brown bear became the hunter and the Nepali was lucky to escape with his life, although he was badly clawed. Jimmy, who had received no formal surgical training, tackled the delicate operation of restoring torn cheek and the jawbone. The boy was now recovering in a nearby ward, his arm joined to his cheek until the graft took and the arm was released.

From the medical point of view working in Nepal can be extremely rewarding. Invariably there are masses of people needing clinical attention of one sort or another, and the astonishing variety of disease and sickness had to be seen to be believed. Shanta Bhawan probably treats only a fraction of the people actually in need of medical attention, as the majority are inland. Even so the influx of those within the environs of Katmandu is such that the hospital is working at peak practically all the time.

I had thought that religious differences would present a major problem, but these are apparently not as great as one might think. It is, however, forbidden by law for a Nepali citizen to convert to Christianity, and nine unfortunate Nepalese were in jail for this reason at the time I arrived in

Shanta Bhawan. I'm afraid that my views on the dissemination of Christian doctrine were at variance with those of some of the militant Christians with whom I discussed the matter.

Nepal is fairly evenly divided between Buddhists and Hindus. I was happy to see any Hindus so inclined become Christians, especially as I found their sacrificial practices abhorrent. The Buddhists, however, and particularly Buddhist Sherpas, were an entirely different matter, and I would certainly oppose the introduction of Christianity into the Solu Khumbu.

In general I like what little I have seen of Buddhism as practiced among the Sherpas. It seems suited to the pattern of living of mountain peoples and has much less of a strangle hold on the Sherpa community than on the more conformist Tibetans. Certainly there are aspects of the Buddhist faith that do not appeal to the orthodox Christian. For me the principal barrier to early conversion is undoubtedly the repulsive and wholly unmelodic beating of drums and blowing of horns that accompanies even the most prosaic of Buddhist functions. This, almost alone, ensures the irrevocable retention of my Christian beliefs. There are elements of the infinite about a faith that has inspired the glorious music of Handel and Bach, yet has retained its humility, regardless of the modern doctrine "In God we trust, all others must pay cash."

I was amused at the attitude of some of the wealthy Hindu patients at Shanta Bhawan. The Hindus saw no reason why they should honor their financial obligations to doctors and hospitals, for, according to the law of karma, the Christian doctors were only helping those less fortunate than themselves, so that they may in turn attain purity of their own souls.

Thus, as products of their past deeds, they were automatically helping themselves toward a better and more fruitful reincarnation by helping others. The Hindu patients, therefore, see little merit in the doctors additionally presenting their bills, when their great reward will be eventual nirvana and eternal peace.

This laudable though inconvenient point of view is of little help to the hospital, which depends for its existence on contributions from overseas and to a less extent from those able and willing to pay for services rendered.

There are other hospitals in the Katmandu Valley, but the greatest source of opposition to Shanta Bhawan is the Hindu faith in the muddy qualities of the Bhagmati, the sacred river flowing through Katmandu toward the greater Ganges. People with all manner of diseases may be seen bathing in the river awaiting a cure, and the ultimate hope and joy of those perilously sick is to die with their feet immersed in the sacred waters. Sometimes elderly people can be seen sitting for days by the banks of the river awaiting release. Their relatives usually gather about them, patiently ready, when death divorces the soul from the body, to light the funeral pyre and immolate the remains. Bands of professional mourners and itinerant musicians offer their services along the stone banks of the burning ghats, while pilgrims from the farthest corners of India throng the temple opposite the sacred hill of Pashupati.

Pashupatinath, the holiest temple of the Lord Siva, embraces the Bhagmati, which flows shallowly through the temple ground, past the golden bull on its carved pedestal. The eight-foot bull, traditional steed of Siva, sits with its gilded backside directed toward the ornamental temple gates, through which no Christian may enter.

Several Hindu patients who might otherwise have lived have died through the determination of their relatives to take them, at any cost, to the Bhagmati. For example, a seriously ill young woman requiring an operation lay in a room near mine. As usual she had been brought to the hospital in the later stages of sickness and in such a weakened condition that an operation could not be performed until she was stronger.

With care and intravenous feeding she had almost reached an operable stage, when the relatives arrived. The doctor sahibs had been given plenty of time to save her and she was no better. Clearly she was going to die and her case for a more fortuitous transmigration would be immeasurably improved if she died within sight of the Bhagmati. There was nothing the doctors could do, because they have no authority to keep an unwilling patient, and they had to let her be carried out. Three days with one's feet in the Bhagmati would kill a normally healthy person, never mind a sick one, and, needless to say, she expired. Her death was undoubtedly hastened by the why-waste-good-food-on-her attitude of the relatives, who were sure that she was about to die anyway.

Relatives can be a mixed blessing, as much in the East as in the West.

Because the hospital usually fed only those patients who could pay for their meals, most of those kept overnight in the wards were fed by their families. Free accommodation was provided for friends and relatives within the hospital grounds by open-fronted brick cubicles, each with a fireplace and a cooking and sleeping area. Often the relatives were away during the day working, but in the evening people from every part of Nepal might be seen around the cooking fires. There were Sherpas and Tibetans from the Buddhist northern valleys, and Tamangs, Limbus, and Rais from the nearby hills. From the Mahabharat ranges came the Magars, Kiratis, the Sunwars and the Gurungs, and from the jungles of the Terai the Dhimals, Kishetriyas, Musalmans, and the Marwaris.

These colorful Buddhist and Hindu peoples live together and happily coexist, each drawing the same inspiration and strength from a belief comparable to that faith which periodically effects the miracles at Lourdes.

ELEVEN

Pethidine Pete

Hon'ble Peter Sahib. I am really so sad to hear how you are sick. I am very much thankful to you for so many things you gave me and also for your kind behaviour towards me. I pray God that you may recover from your sickness. . . . I hope to you will surely respond to this letter.

Yours most obidient servant,
Dawa Thondup

ON MY RETURN FROM THE OPERATING THEATER, with my right hand bound like a badly shaped baseball bat, I found Dawa Thondup's letter slipped under the pillow. I also found a letter from Ed Hillary telling me that he would be in Katmandu in a few days. Dawa Thondup, who could neither read nor write, had paid the Namche Bazar village scribe to write his letter for him. I had not seen Dawa since he ashamedly turned back at Camp III, blinded by headaches and sick from altitude. He was sent to work in the lower camps and eventually moved over to the Silver Hut, so we missed each other, but I expected him in Katmandu soon with Hillary.

His letter, full of concern, moved me greatly, and I dictated a reply first thing next morning. Unfortunately, as there was no runner leaving for Namche Bazar for several days, Dawa arrived at the hospital before the note could be sent. He was overjoyed to receive it and his eyes filled with tears as he rushed off to have it translated, for he had believed that I had forgotten him.

Light rain had fallen during the day, and now the evening air was cool and sweet. The still-wet branches of the giant jacaranda spread a filmy pattern of mauve blossom before my window, small birds chased invisible insects, and below in the darkness a lion roared.

Had I been in Cape Town, I suppose I would have taken it as a matter of course, but in a country where, as far as I knew, there were no lions I thought this decidedly odd. I lay quietly for a moment collecting my thoughts. I knew that hallucinations were a major qualification for the booby hatch —"A lion roaring? Oh yes, I'm *sure* you heard it, we *all* hear these things," they would say with a terrifying attempt at a reassuring smile, clicking their fingers behind their backs as a cue for the entry of two large men in white coats. On the other hand it might just be the pethidine. If it could cause me to imagine that I so vividly heard a lion roar, there was no telling what else it might do.

I was just turning this over in my mind when the lion roared again, this time twice. That settled it: I had at last gone mad and I howled for Sister Fleming. She came rushing in. She told me that it really was a lion, a particularly old and tiresome beast who lived in a cage on a nearby estate. He was a last relic of the Ranas' ostentatious living, nearly all of whom had had their own private zoos. Most nights after that I heard his crusty roar, and although I never met him he became quite a friend and I missed him on the nights he was silent. In a way, I suppose, we had something in common.

Jim Milledge arrived from Khumjung and came up to my room one day to talk about my X-ray plates, which he had been studying with Jimmy Dick. The X-rays clearly showed fluid between the rib cage and my lung, and Milledge considered that this should be drawn off as soon as possible.

As the hospital was short of drugs, Jim decided that a brave fellow like me would be pleased to do without. This, of course, was quite erroneous, as I would cheerfully have soaked up a basinful of morphine had I been given the opportunity. With no chance to defend myself Jim whipped me onto my side and with the consummate skill and relish of an old-time Roman gladiator plunged a needle that felt like an eight-foot javelin into my back. I gave a howl of anguish and spoke to him pointedly, whereupon he gave the javelin a thoughtful twist and remonstrated with me for being rude. Fortunately I was able to draw strength from a sea-man's colorful vocabulary and quickly enlarged upon my previous remarks. Jim grew pale under this onslaught but remained cheerful and continued to ply the bloodstained javelin with vigor. At last it was over, and I was left flapping like a stunned mullet while Jim triumphantly waved a quarter jar of nauseating greenish fluid aloft, the contents, apparently, of my lung. I swore aloud that he should never touch me again, and recommended that he stick to horses, but in fifteen minutes all was well and I felt much relieved.

Shanta Bhawan was, in fact, desperately short of every kind of modern drug, and I had already made heavy inroads into their scanty pethidine supplies. It was difficult to have drugs cleared by Indian customs. They allowed only so much through per year and it was even more difficult to bring medical supplies into Nepal, for reasons best known to the Nepalese Government. The strain on the hospital's resources was considerably relieved in this case by assistance from the New Zealand High Commission in New Delhi, whose staff arranged the transfer of a small package of analgesics sent by the Naval Hospital in Auckland.

Without warning one day Hillary arrived after a fast march out from Khumjung. Bronzed and fit-looking, he gave no evidence of his illness on Makalu and was obviously completely recovered.

He and Jim Milledge, who had generously agreed to forgo his chances on the mountain, had returned to Thyangboche via a low-level, circuitous route down the Barun. In fifteen vigorous days over steep ridges, precipitous gorges, and foaming torrents they never once went above 15,000 feet. Hillary, with his customary resiliency, was soon as strong as ever, but by keeping to fairly modest altitudes he wisely

avoided encountering similar conditions of strain too soon.
He and Milledge arrived in Thyangboche on May 29 in
time to help with the final evacuation of the assault parties
and to supervise the completion of the Khumjung school.

The school project came about when Hillary once asked
two senior Sherpas what they would like most, assuming that
he ever had an opportunity to help them. They were unani-
mous: what they wanted was a chance for their children to
be educated. This greatly interested Hillary, who had felt
that it would be far better to leave the Sherpas alone; but
progress is inevitable in one form or another, as no society
can stand still, not even in the Himalayas. If changes were to
come to the Solu Khumbu, Hillary hoped they would be
orderly and constructive; the first thing to do, he considered,
was to teach the younger Sherpas to read and write.

This is just the sort of project that suits Hillary's talents
for organization, and he hoped, once the first school was
started, to concentrate on the primary needs of the Sherpas,
medical care and agricultural aid. To help start the program,
the sponsors of the expedition, the World Book Encyclopedia,
who are part of the Field Enterprises Educational Corporation, of Chicago, readily gave an initial donation of seven
thousand dollars. Hillary was pleased with the early progress
of the school and intended that Tem Dorje, the Darjeeling-
trained Sherpa teacher, should take the first pupils to about
Standard Four level so that they could become teachers
themselves. As he pointed out, "It would be a bad thing to
overeducate the Sherpas. The Indians and other Asians have
made this mistake—given their young people education and
nothing to do with it. They have thus turned their people
from the land and made them dissatisfied. The result is they
have nothing better to do than stir up unrest."

That education could ever be a liability is a difficult con-
cept for us, but here, where it has little application to the
daily lives of the people, it serves only to make them unhappy with their lot and drive them from the land, which in

turn foments political unrest. Only history can tell if this is ultimately a good thing—at best it is an unhappy form of progress.

The object of the school is to help the Sherpas adapt to their changing environment and to help them have a fuller life through their own efforts and resources. Like most mountaineers, I shared Hillary's tremendous regard for the Sherpas, and I was proud that we, who owed the Sherpas most, should be so closely associated with the project. New Zealand is itself involved in Colombo Plan aid to Nepal, including a milk-treatment plant in Katmandu and a grasslands scheme in west Nepal, assistance that is much appreciated by the Nepalese Government. Here, then, is a chance for New Zealand (and other countries and agencies) to extend these activities by supplementing and supporting Hillary's one-man foreign aid program—a program organized by one of our most able and distinguished New Zealanders, one that doubtless would find favor with the majority of his countrymen, many of whom have had close and lasting contact with the Nepalese peoples, ranging from the Sherpas of the Solu Khumbu to the sturdy Gurkhas of military fame.

Hillary had one piece of news that particularly delighted me and sent my thoughts racing home. He was arranging with the expedition's principals in Chicago for my wife to be flown to Katmandu. It had become increasingly clear that I would have to return to New Zealand on a stretcher and would need some nursing care for the journey. There had been conflicting reports in the home papers, and as yet my wife did not know the true nature of my injuries. I hoped that she would not be shocked by my battered condition.

The hospital pace began to quicken with Hillary's arrival, and activity ebbed and flowed as various friends and expedition members visited my room. Sometimes, heavily sedated, I took little interest in my visitors, but often I could talk for long periods and looked forward to news of home. One afternoon a tall, graying, distinguished-looking gentleman wandered quietly into my room. Unheralded and unannounced, he was the New Zealand High Commissioner to India, Sir Guy Powles. He was visiting Katmandu and was to give a small cocktail party that evening for the expedition. Conscious that I would be unable to attend, he took the trouble to pay me a visit and to remind me that I was not forgotten. I deeply appreciated his thoughtfulness and was later charmed to meet Lady Powles and Mr. and Mrs. McGregor, members of Sir Guy's staff. His attitude contrasted sharply with that of the British Ambassador of the time, who nominally represented New Zealand in Nepal but who took pains to ignore us completely. We found it hard to receive interested and enthusiastic co-operation from the American and Indian representatives in Katmandu when only grudging acceptance was proffered by the British Ambassador. Maybe he had the well-bred Britisher's horror of wild colonial boys.

One morning Marge Dennis arrived with a few tins of lemon drink, and I noticed that she looked unusually pale and quiet. A Nepali friend had found a baby girl, only a few days old and barely alive, on the banks of the Bhagmati and had brought it to her in the early hours of the morning.

Shocked, she had done all she could, but the child had died and was buried that morning. She told me that this was by no means uncommon. Of late she had interested herself in a small clinic designed to rescue and succor unwanted children. She had quickly found herself swamped with children, all girls, for only boys are wanted and can be expected to command a wedding dowry and provide a strong plowing arm.

In some parts people living along the banks of the river shared their paralyzingly poor plot of land with myriads of mosquitoes and were in consequence riddled with malaria and filaria. So poor are they that they are unable to move to better land, and the advent of a girl child is regarded as a disaster. It is from these people that newborn children found at the river largely come. Marge told me that almost every day babies were found abandoned but only rarely alive.

I was told one horrifying story by an eyewitness American
friend which I could scarcely credit. She was crossing a
bridge near the outskirts of Katmandu when she heard
screams from a knot of people gathered near the center of
the bridge. Rushing forward to see what the noise was about,
she recoiled, appalled at the terrible spectacle before her. A
young Nepali woman stood, leaning far out over the wooden
railing of the bridge. In her left hand she held by the foot
the bloody remains of a newborn babe, while with her right
she slashed at it with a long curved kukri.

A more terrible and unnerving scene than this is difficult
to imagine—and the impression that it must have left upon a
lone European woman would be lifelong. I was interested to
hear that, apart from the immediate local disturbance caused
by the incident, it went practically unnoticed by the remainder of Katmandu. This should not be considered strange in a
country where the worst crime imaginable is to kill a cow.
As it is relatively easy to be rid of an unwanted child in
Nepal, it is difficult to explain this particularly bizarre case,
although it was probably a result of postnatal depression, an
unusual and isolated one at that.

Of the principal diseases found in Nepal one of the most
difficult to treat is hookworm. Not that a cure is unknown,
in fact it is a disease that is fairly readily cured, but the trouble is rather one of reinfection. No sooner is a family cured
and returned to their village than the little hanger-on is back
on the job, gaining entry through the sole of the foot, and
soon making himself at home in the small intestine. The problem lies mainly in the Nepalese habits of going barefoot and
attending to their toilet in the middle of the road. One of the
most unpleasant aspects of the journey to Everest is the
necessity to pass through several villages on the outskirts of
Katmandu. Here the areas around the houses and along the
bridle track abound with both human and dog feces.

As Norman Hardie remarks elaborately, "One's olfactory

senses discern the locality of a village before the optic, and one is well advised to walk with care."

The parasite may enter the body in drinking water or through polluted foods, but in the majority of cases it does so by burrowing into the skin, usually through the soles of the feet. Carried by the blood vessels, the worm makes its way to the throat, where it is swallowed, thus reaching the intestines, where it passes out of the body. With the right condition of heat and moisture the larvae then hatch in enormous numbers. Children are affected more than adults, although the disease is common to both, malnutrition being a predisposing factor. We often saw the victims, who were easily recognizable by the distended abdomen, puffy eyes, and general weakness and debilitation. Discussing hookworm with Jimmy Dick, I was surprised to learn that the disease was once so prevalent in the United States that as many as two million cases of hookworm disease existed in the Southern states at one time.

Needless to say we took great care always to wear sand shoes around the environs of Katmandu, as the friendly hookworm knows no distinction of creed or color.

Most evenings I was bothered by strange-looking banded mosquitoes who seemed to be running a private war against me. During the day they hid in various places around the room, preparing themselves for the nightly feasting. With the coming of evening battle commenced, but with my hands bandaged I was at a tactical disadvantage and the evening's honors showed that the bites received grossly outnumbered the mosquitoes slapped. This went on for a few days, with the enemy drawing on hidden reinforcements until my morale weakened and I gradually lost the will to fight. Suddenly all was changed. I was presented with a plastic bug bomb and, seizing the initiative, I was able to perform the happy dispatch before my dazed opponents had time to pull up their landing gear. I had them laid in a row on the window ledge, where they were finally carried away in triumph by a carnivorous gang of marauder ants.

I judged by the lack of mosquito nets that malaria was not a major problem in Katmandu itself, although in the Terai, the low-lying area of jungle between Nepal and India, the yearly malarial death rate is as high as thirty thousand. A possible danger from the type of mosquito that plagued me is filaria, the dread elephantiasis. One does not normally contract the disease from a single bite, but if one is bitten many times over a long period the chance of infection is very high. Again the offender is a parasitical worm that lives in the human body's lymph glands and connective tissue. The young worms produced in the body live in the blood stream; thus, when a mosquito bites an infected person, it takes up the young worms from the blood. The larvae thrive in the mosquito and are transferred from its beak when it bites another man. The worms develop and the female worms and eggs settle in the lymphatic glands, blocking the flow of lymph. The affected organs swell, causing elephantiasis.

I saw few cases of the disease, although I believe it is quite common in Nepal. I remember one middle-aged man who was frequently seen in and around the hospital grounds with a left leg so swollen below the knee that he could barely walk. He contracted the disease as a young man and had suffered several attacks. Each attack left the leg more swollen than before, so that finally it became permanently enlarged. Characteristically, the skin of the affected leg was rough like the hide of an elephant. No doubt this appearance of the skin, coupled with the dimensions of the affected part, gave the disease its name. It was possible to give him some relief with drugs, but as yet there is no known cure for elephantiasis.

For several days I had noticed the smell from my right hand, and although no one mentioned it, it was obvious to me that when anyone came into the room he soon became aware of the sickly sweet odor issuing from within the bandages. It began to worry me a good deal, and upon investigation I found that it came mainly from the thumb and first finger. Below the first joint of each digit a ring of flesh had broken away, leaving the ends shrunken and brittle with an unpleasant line of black gangrenous flesh showing, drawn away from the exposed bone.

I felt a wave of revulsion sweep over me, but now curiosity and concern for the condition of my damaged fingers impelled me to investigate further. Trembling a little, I apprehensively gripped the last segment of the thumb of my left hand. I twisted slightly and immediately broke into a cold sweat. In a wave of sickening horror I realized that the final segments of both the thumb and forefinger were free at the joint and were practically ready to fall off. How can I describe my feelings as I realized that this was just the beginning? I had recently brought myself to face the certain loss of my toes. Could I now adjust myself to this new discovery sufficiently to hide my fear from June, who would shortly arrive in Katmandu? Every finger of both hands was badly scarred with frostbite and I had a dreadful fear that I might lose them all.

Jimmy Dick decided that the time had come to clean up the right hand now that separation had taken place, and the following morning I found myself once again in the operating theater.

After the operation I found that the ends of the middle and ring fingers had had to be amputated, so that the only whole digit on the right hand was the little finger, and it was twisted by the scarred tendon. Naturally I was distressed at the turn of events, but once the useless flesh and bone were cut away, the fingers for the first time began to heal.

As usual mail seemed to take longer getting from India to Nepal than from New Zealand to India, and with no news from home I was beginning to get somewhat edgy. Then, to my surprise, the postal officials surpassed themselves and delivered a telegram. June was in India and had already emplaned for Katmandu.

To my great joy and relief she arrived on time and immediately took over the task of looking after me. This greatly reduced the strain on the hospital staff, who were already working long hours. June lived in the small guesthouse directly outside my window, so close that on still nights we could talk to each other quite comfortably from our rooms. What luxury after the timid roarings of a superannuated lion! Hillary, who was still clearing up the tail end of the expedition, left for Calcutta. There he intended to arrange transport from Katmandu to Calcutta with Air India and the flight back to New Zealand.

In the meantime June was to learn the gentle art of giving painless injections so that she could handle my medication on the long flight to New Zealand. She started her instruction by walking around the wards with Sister Fleming, giving the daily penicillin injections. Wearing a white shirt back to front and clutching a tray of hypodermics, she certainly looked the part, and as evidence of her skill informed me that she was referred to by some as the memsahib doctor. Carried away by the success of this mild deception, June announced that she was now ready to perform her first major operation, and set the date for first thing next day.

The ceremony was performed with due solemnity before a gathering of most of the staff. With a plunge that practically pinned my arm to my chest the first injection was made, and I officially passed into the care of my wife for the journey home.

June's arrival in Katmandu stirred up some interest from the two-page government-controlled newspaper, which sent its only newshawk around for an interview. This *doyen* of the reporting fraternity appeared to slumber through the greater part of the interview, but occasionally demonstrated his attention to detail by asking a series of rapid-fire questions, many of which were irrelevant. He subsequently wrote such a harrowing account of the attempt on Makalu that I had difficulty in recognizing it as the same mountain. The article was headed "Mulgrew's Consolation," which for some reason failed to amuse June.

Near Shanta Bhawan the Swiss Red Cross had begun the construction of one-room brick houses similar to those in the grounds of the hospital. These were to house Tibetan refugee families, whose numbers increased daily in Katmandu. In order to provide some measure of self-support the Swiss were encouraging them in the manufacture of hand-woven Tibetan carpets, which were much sought after in India. June and a missionary friend went to visit the project director, Dr. Toni Hagen. They brought back a sad tale of misfortune and tragedy.

Initially everything had progressed well. A large number of Tibetans were settled and began to work in groups, some preparing wool, others weaving the bright, attractively patterned carpets. Suddenly several were struck down by an infectious disease. They developed swollen carbuncles on their skin, followed by fever, dysentery, and convulsions. Within forty-eight hours two women were dead. The disease was thought to be anthrax, passed on to the Tibetans from infected wool. The only way to prevent further outbreaks of the disease was to burn all the collected wool and vaccinate those as yet unharmed.

As if this were not enough for the struggling community, a further mysterious disease struck, killing five children. Doctors from Shanta Bhawan were hurriedly sent for and quickly diagnosed the disease as nephritis, an inflammation of the kidneys. More difficult to decide was what had caused the disease and why it had attacked only the young children.

Most of the younger people working at the hospital were American students engaged in a variety of jobs, ranging from electricians to kitchen assistants. They were all members of various church groups who chose two years overseas service with the mission rather than compulsory military service.

These young people appeared to work hard and were all popular with the hospital staff. I noticed that they lived frugally and most were taking pains with colloquial Nepali, an indication of their sincere desire to help the people. Some of the group had formed a small choir and one evening gathered in my room to sing hymns. Jammed in like the crowded occupants of a railway carriage, they sang beautifully, beginning with "The Lord's My Shepherd" and finally bringing tears to my eyes with the sailors' hymn "For Those in Peril on the Sea."

About this time I had a fearful row with Christine Eggars, an American nursing sister who had temporarily changed places with Miss Fleming, who was teaching Nepali nurses in another part of the hospital. Christine was deeply concerned about my consumption of drugs and urged me to do everything in my power to reduce them. She pointed out that she was having difficulty in finding a clear spot for the regular injections, as both my arms were sore and she doubted if there was enough flesh on the other obvious place to warrant her trying the needle there. This was true, as both my upper arms were swollen and hard from over four hundred injections, but I was painfully thin everywhere else. She argued that, no matter how strong-willed I thought I was, pethidine would win in the end; it was simply a question of time. Even though I suffered constant pain without it, she urged me to begin reducing the dose or before long, she warned, I would become completely dependent on the insidious stuff.

"Rather than Peter Sahib it will be Pethidine Pete," she said. I took an instant shine to her after this remark and mumbled something about her mind resembling a dismantled bird's nest. This reduced her to tears and me to misery, and it took another day before we could bring ourselves to make it up again. The incident was unfortunate and entirely my own fault, for Chris was only trying to make me see how dangerous the drug could be. The trouble was that I had supreme confidence in my own will power and had no doubt that I could give up pethidine whenever I chose so to do. Anyway, I had discovered an interesting and revelationary aspect of pethidine which absorbed much of my thought. With no difficulty and without the need for virtuous acts of self-denial, it had fallen within my power to become the Dalai Lama himself. Apart from the relief of pain the drug transcended all earthly boundaries and for an hour or so I became the master of my destiny, assuming the shape and purpose of the deity himself if I chose.

Christine Eggars' warning was prophetic indeed.

TWELVE

Return to New Zealand

The Doctors, tender of their fame,
Wisely on me lay the blame.
"We must confess his case was nice,
But he would never take advice.
Had he been ruled, for aught appears
He might have lived these twenty years.
For when we open'd him we found,
That all his vital parts were sound."

Jonathan Swift

HILLARY RETURNED, jaded from the steamy heat of Calcutta and angry at the lack of co-operation from the Nepali Customs. Stores and expedition equipment still lay in wild profusion at Gaucher Airport, when by now they should have been well on the way to India.

Nepal had only recently discovered the joys of the customs shed and was obviously determined to exploit this newfound gift of the Western world to the full. By an intensely thorough and morbidly personal inspection of each single item of equipment and apparel, the customs officials seem set on reducing the visitor to a state of frenzied desolation. Then, after a suitable interval and with unimaginable cunning, a mountainous pile of documents is produced, all written in Nepali script. These, the official explains with deceptive charm, must be completed in triplicate and stamped in Singha Durbar, the government offices, five miles away. Thus ensues a further two weeks of frigid politeness on the part of the visitor as he unhappily tramps from office to office, and cheery nonchalance by various officials, none of whom have the authority to stamp the documents anyway.

Finally the right man is located by an underling, but too late to prevent him from leaving for Pokhara, where he will be for at least two days. This final straw, only the great

Gautama Buddha himself could have withstood impassively, and the shaken visitor retreats to his dusty boxes, sunk in such depths of moral turpitude that he never recovers, and returns home a broken man.

This is the invariable fate of those who travel in the East and who have neither influential friends nor the good sense to slip the customs inspector a new camera or other such bauble at the outset, thereby reducing the pain one hundredfold. Fortunately, Hillary had influence in high places and word of our troubles filtered through to King Mahendra. As though by magic our difficulties dissolved and the previously stony and uphill path became smooth and uncluttered. The bulk of the interminable forms was removed and with their removal vanished even our smallest problems. Cameras, radio transmitters, medical and scientific equipment, tents and personal gear, all began to flow with ceaseless abandon toward Calcutta, and those officials who at first appeared implacable and deadly foes at once became our nearest and dearest friends.

Da Tenzing, Urkein, Annulu, and Dawa Thondup called at the hospital to say farewell. They were tired of the bustle and heat of Katmandu and sickened for their homes and the clear air of the high hills. They planned to return early the next morning to Khumjung. Da Tenzing brought a garland of flowers that they placed about my shoulders, and Dawa Thondup presented me with two sets of hand-embroidered Tibetan boots for my wife and children. The hard yakskin soles smelled dimly of rancid butter and human urine, the curing agent. They were placed with care in a goatskin bag and deposited under my bed, from where, encouraged by the monsoon heat of Katmandu, they permeated the pure air of Shanta Bhawan with a healthy mixture of scents, faintly reminiscent of high passes and steep mountains, boiled yak steaks and dirty feet. Da Tenzing placed his gnarled hands on either side of my forehead with an earnest significance that for the moment escaped me. As they turned to leave, Annulu pressed a small, beautifully wrought, circular brass Tibetan calendar into my hand.

With our customs difficulties at an end and the expedition members taking their various ways home, Hillary was free to, leave. BOAC advised that they were prepared to fly me as a stretcher case from Calcutta to Sydney and TEAL promised to arrange the final leg home to Auckland.

Jimmy Dick agreed that the time had come to leave, as I was now strong enough to stand the journey. With a new development, septicemia in my left foot, he urged better hospital facilities as soon as possible. While I knew that a move to a larger hospital was necessary and urgent, I was profoundly aware of the devotion and skill that had been given me at Shanta Bhawan. What my fate might have been had this Christian outpost not existed does not bear thinking of.

For the last time I was carried down Shanta Bhawan's marble staircase, not unexpectedly, headfirst. The hospital's brand new motor ambulance stood at the main entrance surrounded by a throng of Nepali friends and relatives waiting expectantly in the courtyard. Although the valley was filled with clouds, I caught a glimpse of the glittering peak of Dorje Lhagpa standing proud against a cobalt-blue backdrop, with the landscape below spreading clear in golden sunlight.

Nurses and patients crowded the windows and balconies waving and shouting. Fresh-cut garlands of flowers were placed about my neck, heavy scented and overpowering, the moist colors staining the white hospital jacket. A last wave, the doors closed and the long journey home began.

The ambulance, a gift of British make, had arrived only the day before, and the Newar driver, seizing the opportunity, drove all the way to the airport with the siren howling. This innovation on the Katmandu scene sent people, bicycles, chickens, dogs, and children scattering in all directions and set an immediate and unassailable record from hospital to airport.

At the airport we were met and farewelled by General Kaiser, a leading Nepali official in the King's advisory service. All our American friends were there, and several expedition Sherpas, savoring still the delights of Katmandu, appeared in a hapless Jeep that drove to a stop on the tarmac, boiling furiously and emitting a curious roaring sound amid clouds of vapor. Designed to carry six in a pinch, the invisible vehicle disgorged at least a dozen steamed, crumpled Sherpas headed by Gumi Dorje, the Sherpa who had suffered a transverse fracture of the leg on Ama Dablam. I was pleased to see so many friends and sorry to say good-by, but the weather was poor and the pilot was anxious to be away. We made the flight to Calcutta in a battered Dakota of Nepali Airlines. I remember little of it, for I was sedated, for the time being related to the Dalai Lama.

The aircraft was full of heavily armed Gurkha soldiers returning to their posts in the foothills near the Indian border. I awoke to an almost empty plane just as we rolled to a stop on Dum Dum Airfield. The soldiers had mysteriously gone and only June, Ed, and a couple of passengers remained. I was carried from the plane and placed on a stretcher in the shade of the wing. It was a burning-hot afternoon, and I began to wilt as a dozen or so Indian reporters with cameras fell over one another taking photographs. Hillary stepped in and restored order, waving over an ancient ambulance parked near the edge of the runway.

We rattled along the familiar route toward the center of Calcutta. Lying on my back, I could see little, but there was no need, for a hundred sounds and smells told me of our progress. Through the disheveled cantonments surrounding the airport we went, horn blowing incessantly and the vehicle swaying back and forth as we dodged about the crowded streets. Beggars cried for attention and sticky fruit sellers called their wares. Children, dogs, cows, bustle, and dust, heat and smell—all familiar and distinctive sounds of the Indian city. Past dilapidated bungalows and into the tourist streets with their Victorian buildings we went, past jewelers' shops and clothing and leathercraft stalls. Merchants in Western-style jackets stood at their doors, and peasants with once-white dhotis around their legs rubbed shoulders with over-clothed tourists, tired and perspiring but intent on their "round the world in ten days" tour.

June and I spent the night in a private hospital sporting the improbable name of Middleton Mansions. It was staffed mainly by Anglo-Indian nurses, with an English matron in charge and an English resident doctor.

I had a room to myself, but because it was a very small one June was given a bed upstairs, in the maternity ward. It occurred to me that this might be tempting providence unnecessarily, but she was resolute and insisted on remaining in the hospital overnight.

BOAC made special arrangements for the long flight to Sydney. Although a stretcher could not be used I was carried into the plane, where I was made fairly comfortable. Every four hours June produced her little hypodermic with professional aplomb, reducing my jangled nerves to a state of quiet tranquillity and the passengers to one of frenzied admiration. With the exception, that is, of an elderly German lady who viewed the proceedings with grave suspicion and who created a mild disturbance every time the "fasten seat belts" light came on, by walking up and down the aisle like an expectant father. She occupied most of her time eying us with the detached air sometimes adopted by high court judges. We became uncomfortable under her vigilant gaze. Ed assumed an attitude of studied indifference. This was designed to give the impression that he invariably traveled with bearded, wild-looking characters closely resembling Ben Gunn escaped from Treasure Island.

At Singapore, Hillary considered having a break and stopping the night, but I found the lifting in and out of the plane worse than the long flight, and we decided to push on and get it over. A few hours from Darwin the heat, cramped conditions, and general fatigue hit me and my legs began to ache miserably. They gradually got worse and nothing June was able to do seemed to make any difference. Ed had a word with the pilot, who radioed ahead asking the airways doctor to meet the plane on arrival in Darwin.

The plane touched down shortly after 2 A.M. on a dark, rain-soaked tarmac. We were pleased to be in Australia, regarded by New Zealanders as almost back on home soil but I was not up to smiling much, as I expected a pretty unenthusiastic reception from the doctor, who had probably been pulled out of bed in the rain. As the last of the passengers filed out, I heard a lovely Australian twang inquire of the steward, "Where's this Himalayan horse you've got aboard, mate?"

A cheery, barrel-chested man wearing crisp white shorts came down the aisle followed by a scarlet-caped nursing sister carrying the doctor's traditional badge of office, a small black bag. It was a reception completely opposite to what I had expected and it came as a breath of fresh air to June and me. Nothing was too much trouble, and with evident sympathy Doc promised to put me to sleep for the next leg of the journey, the long hop to Sydney.

Talking all the while, he produced a lethal-looking hypodermic syringe, no smaller than a World War II stirrup pump, which he claimed he had used on a horse only that morning—"Without complaint," he remarked as I cringed back in my seat.

He seemed to have an obsession for horses. Personally, I saw no reason to doubt that he had used the same needle on a horse that morning. Why not? In Darwin he would probably get more horse than human patients. Anyway I survived, and he knew his business, for I slept soundly all the way to Sydney, waking only when two husky Australian ambulance men arrived to carry me out of the plane. I was taken to a small private hospital in Rose Bay, staffed mainly by New Zealand nurses. June and I were received with great kindness by the matron, who locked me away in a single room secure from the reporters who had pestered her ever since the news leaked out that I was expected to spend one night in Sydney.

The Australian press printed some fantastic stories about my survival which could only have come from some erudite reporter's imagination. One report claimed that I had walked the length of the Himalayas with my feet wrapped only in rags.

With the matron and nurses on guard I slept undisturbed, and all remained quiet except for one enterprising reporter who convinced the matron that he was my cousin. She brought him into the room when I awoke, whereupon he revealed his true identity and offered to leave, as he saw that I was in no condition for an interview.

Ed arranged the flight to Auckland with TEAL first class, which meant champagne, thoroughly enjoyed by him and June but, much to my chagrin, not permitted to me. This was the last leg of the long journey home and it was mercifully swift—Sydney to Auckland took only three hours.

Strengthened and fortified with pethidine, I was taken on a stretcher straight to an ambulance drawn up alongside the plane. Surgeon Commander John Reid, from the Naval Hospital, and Gordon Brown, the St. John's ambulance driver, were waiting, and with all customs formalities waived June and I were whisked off to the Devonport Naval Hospital. We were met by the matron, who had prepared a single room in the officers' ward on the top floor. June went off home to Browns Bay to see to our two children, while I relaxed, happy to be home but concerned for the future.

The Naval Board had granted me one year's leave for the expedition, but by edict of the Treasury Department, it was to be taken as leave without pay. When the then Prime

Minister, Mr. Walter Nash, got to hear about the parsimonious attitude adopted by the Treasury, he arranged for me to go on half pay. I appreciated very much this generous reversal of my fortunes, for it enabled June to get by without fear of the bailiff appearing at the door.

Now, however, things might change. I knew that skin grafting was a long and tedious process and I guessed that much would be needed if my feet were to be saved. On the one hand medical treatment in New Zealand is free, but on the other I might reasonably expect to be discharged from the Navy on medical grounds. This would automatically be without a pension, as I was not on naval service when the accident occurred. With all this in mind I was seriously worried. I could see only the dreary prospect of several years on social security payments, at least until I could rehabilitate myself. Filled with gloom and distressed at the probable loss of my career, I passed a sleepless night worrying about the effect this might have on my growing family.

Peace of mind was not improved the next morning when, after an examination by naval doctors, I learned that my right lung had refilled with pus and an operation had become a matter of urgency. I was mulling over this unpleasant piece of news when the naval officer in charge, Auckland, Commodore J. O'C. Ross, walked in. He came straight to the point. He had been instructed by the Naval Board in Wellington to tell me how sorry they were to learn of the accident on Makalu and that no matter what might happen in the future, even should I prove permanently unfit for sea, I would always have a job with the Navy Department. My cup was filled to overflowing, and, as if this were not enough, he added that as from the day I landed back in New Zealand, July 14, 1961, I was officially returned to full pay. I was delighted and babbled my thanks, as all my fears of future unemployment and immediate financial problems disappeared.

Whether it was by chance or design that the Naval Board

178 *Return to New Zealand*

chose that particular day to inform me of their decision I
have never found out, but it was right when I needed it most
and provided a wonderful fillip to my morale. I learned
later that the board knew that I was far sicker than I realized
and that the chances of saving my feet were very slim indeed. The toxins from my lung had spread throughout the
circulatory system to such an extent now that any operation
needed must be done quickly, otherwise I would soon be too
weak to stand major surgery, and without surgery to clear
the lung I might die from accumulated poisons. I knew little
of this but had begun to suspect that I might be confined to
a hospital bed for years. This possibility appalled me. Both
June and I were very anxious for an expert decision as soon
as possible so that we might know what to expect.

The answer was soon to come, for the Navy was as anxious
as we were that a decision be quickly made. I was visited
every day by the director of Naval Medical Services, Surgeon Captain E. McPhail, who made his rounds promptly at
eleven each morning. He was the most kindly and considerate of men with a charming friendly manner that immediately
made me feel at ease. Apart from his professional interest in
my case he spent many hours talking to my wife and helping
us both through the trying period we were now facing. At
the beginning of the second week in the Naval Hospital, Captain McPhail told me that arrangements had been made for
a well-known plastic surgeon to see me. He would decide
what was to be done about my feet and where I should go
for treatment. The captain thought that I might have to go to
Burwood Hospital in Christchurch, where other frostbite
cases had been treated.

I waited impatiently for the expert, whom I knew was regarded as one of the top men in Australasia, and I expected
that whatever the decision he made I could regard as virtually
final. He was held up to me as such a paragon by the hospital
staff that I began to imagine him as a saintly combination of
Albert Schweitzer and Dr. Kildare, one whose miracle touch

would instantly reduce the complex exigencies of my shattered self to one of near bliss.

It was ever thus, and, fact being indisputably stranger than fiction, the great man proved to be the antithesis of all that I had expected. His arrival was heralded by a midmorning flap on the part of matron, who bustled in and rearranged my bedcovers for the fortieth time. The sheets were turned back at the bottom of the bed, exposing my feet so there should be no delay in an instant appraisal and inspection.

The surgeon captain and several other doctors came in and grouped themselves around my bed. I looked expectantly at the door, wondering how a man eight feet tall would manage to get through, when I realized that he was already among us and had begun his inspection.

With the exception of my distinctly tattered self the great man was about the most insignificant-looking person in the room, although clearly the most dominant. At first glance he might have passed for a school inspector or a borough clerk, and, like Miss Haversham, he wore an air of haughty distaste, like an ill-fitting bowler. That the odor from my gangrenous fingers and feet he found nauseating was evident, for he never came closer than four feet from the bed, and he took great care to keep a handkerchief pressed firmly against his olfactory organ the whole time he was in the room. He half-circled the bottom of the bed several times, his attention riveted on my offending feet, while his distinguished colleagues pressed back against the wall, keeping well out of his way. As unimpressed with me as I was with him, he never so much as acknowledged the existence of a human being attached to the distasteful feet, and without a word he shook his bald head in a final gesture of disapproval and departed like the Cheshire cat in *Alice*, leaving a disembodied grimace hanging in the air.

A sense of foreboding and gloom enveloped me. A little banter or a cheering word from the eminent surgeon and I would have felt, even if my worst fears were realized, that my destiny lay in the hands of a friend. Now, after this bout of studied silence and complete lack of communication, mental or otherwise, I felt let down and abandoned.

Perhaps for this reason the blow, when it came, was less heavy but nonetheless shocking. John Reid wasted no time, and as soon as a decision was reached he came straight to my room, his face set in such a serious expression that I knew even before he spoke that he brought bad news.

"The consultant is of the opinion that plastic surgery is out of the question," Reid said. "Even if it were attempted it would mean three years in hospital with an almost certain chance of eventual failure and the probability of your becoming a permanent invalid."

I had no need to ask it, but the question came almost automatically, "What's the alternative?"

"Amputation of both feet," said Reid grimly. The verdict was out. It was not unexpected, but I still refused to accept it and told Reid that I would never permit such an operation.

"Even if you stick out for skin grafting," he said, "the consultant is not prepared to tackle it, as he considers the chances of success too slim."

This was the final blow. If the acknowledged expert refused to operate, then I was given no choice and, whatever I might think at the moment, I must eventually come around to agreeing to amputation. I waited anxiously for lunchtime, when I knew that June would arrive for her afternoon visit. How could I expect the doctors, or anyone else for that matter, to understand the tragedy that amputation represented for me. To most of them mountaineering was a strange and unnecessarily hazardous sport, and few knew anything of the pleasures or of those elusive qualities of the high hills which defy analysis and quicken the blood. I counted myself fortunate to have trodden the heights of the Himalayas, to have sat with friends by campfires in the New Zealand bush, and to have sledged across the desolate antarctic. The imperishable memory of these things would always remain with me, but I was aghast at the finality of amputation, which would irrevocably end my participation in such great adventures forever.

I was now able to see why, a few days previously, Dr. David Cole was so amused when we were discussing the forthcoming operation on my lung. He told me that it would be necessary to remove a very small portion of rib, which caused me to be desperately worried at the effect it might have on any future mountaineering I might do. No wonder he laughed. There I was, concerned at the inconsequential loss of a half inch of rib, while the implications of years in hospital or even death from toxemia had entirely escaped me.

June arrived and as soon as we were alone I told her of the happenings of the past few hours and of the decision I was now called upon to make. Although immensely distressed she never showed it; she was concerned only that we do the right thing as soon as possible, for I was looking progressively worse each day. This I had realized. I was now much weaker than the day we arrived in Auckland, less than two weeks previously. For all our talk and our endless discussion of alternatives and possibilities, we both knew in our hearts that the expert was right, and the sooner we faced the truth the better.

Thinking of all this, now that my wounds are healed by time and surgery, I frequently wonder about the plastic surgeon. Did he avoid making any human contact with me purposefully—in order to give a more dispassionate opinion? At the time of his advent, I was living in an atmosphere of false hope—my own hopes and those of my physicians and friends. Did he have to be a little brutal to clarify the issue? I suppose I may never know. . . .

That afternoon I sent word to the surgeon captain that I agreed to both operations, the rib resection and the amputation of both feet.

THIRTEEN

Look to the Mountains

His fire is out, his wit decay'd,
His Fancy sunk, his muse a jade,
I'd have him throw away his pen,
But there's no talking to some men.

Jonathan Swift

No TIME WAS LOST. Next morning I found myself, accompanied by a pretty Irish nurse, in an ambulance on the way to Greenlane Hospital in Auckland. I was taken straight to Ward 2 under the charge of Sister Gratton and given a small single room at the western end of the ward. There was just space for a chest of drawers and two chairs, but I did not care, as I was alone, and at the time this was important to me.

I was still on two-hourly doses of pethidine, but it had begun to have less and less effect, and after forty minutes or so the pain in both feet would come surging back. It came as a throb at first but quickly rose to an almost unbearable crescendo so that I lay in bed rocking from side to side with a rhythmic motion that seemed to alleviate it a little. It was difficult to remember days with no pain, and the happy days at the beginning of the expedition were so far away in my mind they were now only a dream. The pain in my feet and sometimes in my still-raw fingers nagged in every waking moment. After a while I found it impossible to imagine a future devoid of pain.

Like Chris Eggars, Sister Gratton was extremely concerned about the large doses of pethidine I was being given, but she recognized the need for it at the time, at least until the operations were over.

The first operation, for chronic empyema, was performed by David Cole on the Tuesday after I arrived in Greenlane. I awoke back in my room with a swelling pain in my right side, and taped to the wound was an unruly length of tubing that ran through a vacuum jar to a pump nozzle attached to the wall. Every time I moved the tube sucked like a thirsty python and the discharge jar at the side of the bed rattled and spat as it gradually filled. It was like being permanently attached to a gigantic tapeworm, and I was horrified to learn that he was to be with me for several days and "I might just as well make friends with him."

Easier said than done, for he regularly tugged at the stitches cementing him to the wound, and each time I moved I found myself cursing him and his medical progenitors.

On the following Friday I received a visit from Mr. Harman Smith, a prominent orthopedic surgeon, who was to perform the major operation. I liked him instantly, an affection that dimmed slightly when he told me that, assuming I felt well enough, the operation was planned for the next morning. I already knew this but had hoped that some major cataclysm might remove Saturday from the calendar or, perhaps more to the point, remove Harman Smith. However, the day dawned without any sign of divine intervention and after a premed from a disgustingly cheerful ward sister I was wheeled miserably away to the theater, dragging my tormenting tapeworm after me, gurgling and guggling merrily into his jar, which had to come too. There was a few minutes' delay in the theater for some final preparations. I had time to note the unusually large number of green-gowned people about the table and to fight back a few seconds of momentary panic, when I felt a slight rushing sound in my head and everything went dark.

It was done. I regained consciousness back in my room, vaguely at first and aware only of a heavy feeling about my legs, but conscious at the same time of the white ceiling above two plasma bottles beside the bed. I could no longer remember why I was there but I knew June must be near somewhere. I called out to her and although I heard her voice I was unable to make out what she was saying, nor could I see her. Instead a strange face slowly focused into view beside the bottles.

"You're awake, are you?" said Dr. Graham.

I tried to sit up but nothing happened. I could still not see June but I felt her holding my left hand. There seemed to be a long period of oblivion where I could see nothing but was conscious of movement within the room.

Again Dr. Graham's face appeared, bending low and looking at me quizzically through his spectacles. Now my legs hurt with such a bitter ache that I lost interest in what had happened, or where I was, and could only think of relief from the hammering pain that rapidly grew worse by the minute. I cried to Graham to help me, but he had already injected as much morphine as he dared and could only sit by and tell me to wait, the pain would soon go off.

It didn't, and we both knew why. The huge amounts of pethidine taken in the weeks before amputation had built up such a tolerance that the morphia was having a very limited analgesic effect. The agony increased to the point where my whole body seemed a mass of torn nerves and I saw everything through a crimson glow of pain. I could stand it no longer and watched with fervent hope as Graham, desperate to help, jabbed a hypodermic into the plastic tube of the blood drip connected to a vein in my arm. "The amount you've had in the last hour would kill any normal man," he said. "You should get relief now in a few seconds."

Consciousness slowly withdrew and instead of the legs hurting so much they resumed that heavy leaden feeling. The afternoon wore on and I gripped one of June's fingers so tightly that she was unable to break away. It was long past her time to leave, but she had no option and just had to sit waiting for me to awake and release her finger.

The first few days passed in a half world of drugged stupor, visitors, nurses, and patches of lucid talking, mostly to June, who came each day. From the first Sister Gratton made special arrangements for June to come at any time, and each lunch hour she ate in my room and helped me to get down a little liquid or food.

Slowly the shock subsided, but the pain in my legs was always there, ready to surge back as soon as the injections wore off. I began to watch the clock, counting the minutes until the next shot was due and anxious lest the nurse should be busy and arrive late. Strength gradually returned, but with no leverage from my feet I was often unable to sit up after I had slipped down in the bed. I lay in awkward positions sometimes for long periods, unable to help myself or to reach the bell and summon assistance. That I might show pain when visitors were in the room worried me continuously, and I often asked Sister Gratton to give me an injection when I knew any were expected.

At first this was rare, as only immediate members of my family or very close friends were allowed. Ed Hillary arrived most evenings and we talked over past expeditions and various friends, but the time must have dragged for him, as I often drifted off and forgot he was there. I used to make a mental effort to concentrate, but it rarely worked and my mind would slip away, until sometimes I found myself back once more on Makalu reliving the terrors of that last night at Camp VII.

I began more and more to appreciate visits from friends, but I knew what a trial it must be to them at times. People felt so helpless to do anything for me, and an hour each evening looking at my unresponsive gray face, peering above the great hump of bedclothes over my legs, was not conducive to a cheerful occasion.

The commanding officer of H.M.N.Z.S. *Philomel*, Captain L. G. Carr, a family friend of many years' standing, arrived at the hospital every evening. For this I was profoundly grateful. An immensely thoughtful and considerate man, he worked almost as hard for my recovery as I did, and I owed much to his patience during the first trying weeks.

The accident and its aftermath brought a flood of mail to the hospital, and day after day June read handfuls of letters to me from people all over New Zealand and overseas. I was extremely touched by the warm concern expressed by so many of my fellow countrymen, and I regretted that I was unable to write back personally. Each evening June wrote in reply to the day's mail, but she did not manage to clear the backlog until weeks after I was out of hospital. We had letters from farmers inviting June and the children to holiday with me on their farms from almost every province in New Zealand, and letters from children, many in braille, simply poured in. Many came from amputees anxious to help me get over the difficult stages of learning to walk again. Many people sent us a pound note, often five pounds, and only rarely did we know who the donor was. We were both touched by these examples of spontaneous generosity and have always regretted that we were unable to thank our benefactors.

Ed Hillary brought me a copy of the Douglas Bader story, hoping, no doubt, to inspire me to greater things. Although I was tremendously impressed with his magnificent spirit, I did not take much to the book portrait of the man and felt that he was the sort of person I could heartily dislike without overmuch effort. This reaction was probably due in part to the first few pages of the book, where he was described as "an object for youthful hero worship, dashing airman, brilliant rugger player and cricketer, and vitally handsome." This description made me feel as though I was passing through a par-

ticularly arid stretch in my own hitherto unspectacular
career. I was never much good at cricket anyway.

On the whole I was unable to concentrate on reading and
after an injection I just lay in a stupor until the effects wore
off; then my legs hurt too much to give me any peace. My
parents arrived up from Wellington, and although the meeting was painful for them, I was pleased to let them see that
I was at least alive and for the first time beginning to put on
a little weight.

A welcome visitor was the then Chief of Naval Staff,
Admiral Phipps. I appreciated his taking the time to see me.
Again it was the morale boost that helped so much. He suggested that I might work in the Naval Research Laboratories
at least until I felt fit enough to return to general service.
The fact that he even mentioned general service was enough
for me, as it indicated that I was not regarded as a complete
write-off by the Navy.

At about this time two well-known reporters from an
Auckland evening newspaper talked their way past the ward
sister. They wanted to write a serialized account of the
Makalu attempt, and the paper offered a good financial return. It was tempting to lie back and let someone else do the
writing, but I refused, for several reasons. For one thing, I
was not enthusiastic about an account that would probably
exaggerate the most dramatic aspects of the climb, and for
another I was simply not able to concentrate for more than
a few minutes at a time. As it was, while they were in the
room, I was happily passing through one of my Dalai Lama
phases and kept dropping off to sleep on them. I don't know
how coherent they expected me to be, but they left with the
impression that I had never got past the fourth grade.

I was now feeling quite a lot stronger, and through the
efforts of Mrs. Barr, the hospital almoner, a wheel chair was
produced and for the first time I was able to escape from my
room.

It took some practice hoisting myself out of bed into the

chair but after a day or so I could manage without help and, providing it was within reach, could wheel myself down the ward on interesting little exploratory trips whenever I liked. This new-found maneuverability, while excellent for me, represented a major hazard to Dr. Cole. I was now in a position to pursue him, and with practice I could get him cornered almost before he stepped into the ward. This was brought home to him one morning when I thought that I was being deliberately kept from my 8 A.M. pethidine injection. As soon as he appeared in the ward, I hopped into my chariot and scooted after him, selfishly complaining and demanding the injection. That settled it. He recognized my whimsical little failing as addiction and decided to begin reducing the drug level immediately. The trouble was that he had no way of knowing how much was genuine pain and how much was just a simple need for pethidine.

He knew that after so many weeks of real agony the threshold, or level of pain where it became unbearable, would have decreased to such an extent that a pinprick might seem like a hammer blow to me. However, as no one wanted me to suffer unnecessarily, a gradual reduction plan was implemented. In retrospect, I have always thought this was the time to bring me into the picture and thus give me an opportunity to help myself, but it was not to be. I was aware of the concern, of course—it was obvious—but nobody ever used the word addiction before me, and when I asked directly I was assured that I was not actually addicted but that "we" would have to be careful.

When the hospital started seriously to reduce the drug level, I noticed that now and again I had inexplicable periods of sweating and sleeplessness. I was unable to lie still for more than a few minutes, and often the room seemed to be closing in. Sometimes I felt absolutely unable to meet or speak to people and at others I had an unreasonable fear that something might have happened to June and that I would not see her again. The nights became a torment. One evening I had the hallucination that all the corners of the room were alive with little crawling insects. They vanished when I switched the lights on, but I was astonished at the realism of the impression and could hardly believe that it was only imagination. This particular hallucination occurred just once, but it was enough to give me a bad fright and for the first time I realized I was probably suffering from withdrawal symptoms.

All hospitals have certain well-established routines that are not going to be disturbed by the mere needs of its ailing patients. Early-morning washing of patients, for example, seems to offer a particular delight, especially to those nauseatingly healthy trainee nurses who flit into the room spraying soapy water in all directions and uttering inane banalities on the beauties of the dawn. As I pointed out to Sister Gratton, it was not that I particualrly disliked washing, it was just the unearthly time selected for the performance. Protests made no difference, and they continued the ordeal by suds with all the quiet charm of medieval Chinese water torturers.

Another thing in this catalogue of horrors is porridge. I can't stand it, but the New Zealand medical profession apparently regards it with mystic reverence, and by the regularity of its appearance on my breakfast tray I think they would supply it intravenously if that were possible. It is high time porridge and porridge eaters were placed in their true perspective, high time, too, for authority to recognize that, contrary to popular Scottish belief, there are people who do not turn delirious with joy at the prospect of their national breakfast.

Like Piltdown man, porridge is a gigantic hoax anyway and the Scots have laughed at the world ever since some idiotic Highlander first concocted the gruesome stuff.

I spent almost three weeks in Ward 2. This was longer than usual, as most patients are transferred to a convalescent ward after surgery and removal from the seriously ill list. In my case, instead of convalescing at Greenlane, I was returned to my old room in the Naval Hospital.

June and I were talking in the hospital one morning when Jim Church, the naval consulting surgeon, walked into the room. We chatted for a few moments, and as he was about to leave I said, "Anyway, what am I to do about this drug business?"

The question may have appeared casually phrased, but I had been brooding over the probability of addiction for some days and had determined to ask Church directly the first time I caught him alone.

Church, who is one of the most kindly and understanding men I have met, wasted no time with petty preliminaries. "Well, Peter," he said, "you are addicted, and have been for some time. The sooner you face it and get stuck in and do something about it the better."

Like a shipwrecked sailor clinging to a waterlogged buoy, I struggled against the truth, but it was out and I had no excuse.

Somehow I felt unclean, although reality came as no genuine surprise. Now that I had been told the truth I realized that what I had forced from my mind I had in fact known all along, perhaps even as far back as the last weeks in Katmandu. Now my only thought was to give up the injections as quickly as possible.

June, who had unbounded faith in my will power, had wanted to tell me at Greenlane, but had been asked not to, as it was considered too risky; there was no knowing, she was told, how I might react.

In the afternoon I tackled John Reid, who said that the hospital had been weaning me steadily from pethidine for some time but had not thought it advisable to tell me. I became angry and retorted that I was strong enough to give the whole lot up any time. Why didn't they just try me?

That was enough. The following day everything stopped. No injections, no tablets, no sleeping pills, not even an aspirin, and I hated it. Worse, I hated myself for talking my way into a situation I was not sure I could carry off. Fortunately, the surgeon captain made a wise decision and allowed June to take me home the same day. He felt that among my family I would be happier with more to interest me, and might more easily overcome the withdrawal problems I had now to face.

How can I describe the week that followed or, the worst of it, the first three days? It was cold, wintry weather, with rain squalls frequently blotting out the view of the sea from across the green hills behind the house. I lay on a couch in the front room beside a blazing log fire. At first I was comfortable except for some pain in my legs, but within twelve hours I was unable to keep still. Sweat, not the normal healthy sweat, but sharp, acrid, and unhealthy, exuded from every pore of my body and ran in rivulets down my face.

Each bone seemed to ache individually and I had a compelling desire to do something, anything, just to keep moving. I seemed unable to tolerate any bodily position of rest for more than a few moments, and ordinary light became for a time unendurably brilliant. I had periodic fits of uncontrollable shivering, although the room was quite warm, and at night I slept only in snatches. The nights were a special terror. Time stood still and the hours dragged by while I lay wide-eyed, desperate for sleep but afraid of the dreams that sleep brought.

We had pethidine and hypodermics in the house, but although I often thought of it I managed to so set myself that I never discussed them with June. We eventually handed these back intact to the naval doctors, who would not have let me come home had they known the drugs were in the house.

Sometimes I would torture myself with the thought of what one small injection would do for me, perhaps even only half the usual amount. I almost convinced myself that a last final injection would give me the strength to fight the terrible craving for peace, and relief from the continual bodily ache the craving induced. Had I relaxed sufficiently to allow myself to persuade June to give me one pethidine tablet, there is no doubt that I might never have regained the moral

strength to fight on, and would have slowly slipped hopelessly toward total addiction.

After three days the worst was over and the continual
sweating subsided to a more bearable level. My eyes once
more focused correctly and within another week I knew
that I need no longer worry. The craving, the "needle hap-
piness," had gone and as far as I could tell gone irrevocably.

The pain in my legs, although much lessened, persisted for
a few more weeks, but by now I was almost used to it and
had accepted it. It therefore came as a tremendous shock one
afternoon when, like a clock suddenly stopping in a still
room, the ache vanished. I could hardly believe it. From that
time the pain-free periods, although certainly very short—
perhaps just a few seconds initially—gradually lengthened,
until finally several days went by without any semblance of
pain at all.

The season and the weather changed and most days I was
able to sit outside in my wheel chair, browning in the sun.
Goodhearted friends built a wooden ramp from the house
to the back lawn so that I could wheel myself out whenever
I so desired, and other thoughtful business friends provided
me with a television set. I read so much that I felt as though
I had read every book in the world, and each day I grew
stronger and fatter as I sat in the sun like a complacent
brown blob.

One day a traveling salesman saw me on the lawn and asked
if I had been in a motor accident. To save explanations, I
replied in the affirmative. He nodded and said, "Well, never
mind, old son, it could have been worse, look at the rough
time that bloke Mulgrew had." I cheered inwardly and felt
that I had at last thrown off my other scarecrow self; all I
had to do now was to get out of the damned wheel chair.

To do this and learn to walk again took longer than I had
expected, and at first I despaired of ever managing it. Almost
every day June drove me over to the Disabled Servicemen's
Artificial Limb Centre in Auckland. Here with a wealth of

tact, understanding, and patience the staff worked with me, each week bringing just a little improvement.

Firstly I was introduced to wooden peg legs, or pylons. These were designed to help me regain balance and to shape the stumps so that proper artificial limbs could be fitted. They felt heavy and awkward and the sockets hurt, but at last I saw real progress and I assiduously practiced daily for several weeks. By Christmas of the same year I was ready for the final fitting, and in January 1962 I rather proudly laced on my first pair of new shoes—one size smaller than before.

My hands still worried me a lot. One day the strain of walking while holding onto the wooden walking rail was so great that the partly healed fingers of my right hand burst open and I had to give up for a few days. I determined not to use crutches, and never really needed to anyway. At home I got about by walking around the furniture and holding onto anything handy. It took a long time to summon the courage simply to let go and launch myself across the room, but I knew that I must do it and struggled hard for the necessary confidence. In fact, once I made the effort and went solo, my confidence grew alarmingly and I almost went to the other extreme, trying all sorts of unnecessarily difficult things. With the hurdle of walking unaided over, I practiced on rough ground with the consulting physiotherapist at the Limb Centre. We walked together around the grounds and along the road and occasionally several times around a nearby bowling green. All the while he talked and distracted my attention so that I gave up looking at my feet and learned to look ahead rather than at the few inches of ground immediately in front of me.

It seemed impossible, but gradually balance and a certain amount of natural movement came. Where the legs at first hurt every time I walked, they now gave little trouble, and I was able to concentrate on the small, important things, like the length of step and the correct body movements. I never fell, and although at first I used a stick presented to me by the

Prime Minister, Mr. Holyoake, I soon learned to do without it and rely solely on balance and judgment.

Not falling puzzled me, as I had been told to expect many tumbles. In Bader's story, *Reach for the Sky*, I noticed that he fell frequently, even long after he walked and had learned to play golf. Perhaps I had advantages not always enjoyed by others in the same unwelcome position. I was young and had a mountaineer's natural balance, which I had probably not lost. More important, I was heartened by endless hours of patience from my wife, who never let me overdo it and rush to my own destruction, but who encouraged every fresh step or advance.

Although I had been told otherwise, I was relieved to find that driving the car came fairly readily and with a few days' practice I felt quite confident in traffic. Thank heavens, I thought to myself, I did not accept the kindly meant offer to fit hand controls. Had I done so I would never have known they were unnecessary. Now with the car, and able to walk, life took on a new savor and I began to look forward to returning to work.

I continued to make regular visits to the Limb Centre in Auckland for innumerable leg adjustments and advice, but now with the fingers of both hands healed I was able to make more rapid and confident progress. Weary months still lay ahead, months of constant and diligent practice, but with the passage of time I went from strength to strength. Ultimately, after many months I felt strong enough to return to naval duty and made application accordingly.

A medical board was arranged at the Naval Hospital. To my relief I was given a clearance and permission to begin work at the Naval Research Laboratory the following Monday. This was a great and memorable occasion for me, but an event of more importance and of even greater significance occurred the first evening I arrived home. With my younger daughter on my shoulders I found myself able to walk unaided around the house and up to the front door. There was no tendency to overbalance and no stumbling. For the first time I seemed to have found that combination of balance and co-ordination that we all learn rapidly as children but that since the accident had escaped me.

Often my thoughts return to the mountains. No fate, no cosmic catastrophe can deprive me of the fulsome memories of my mountain days, but I am unable to content myself with that prerogative of cows, the meditative chewing of the cud. I long to experience again the few vitalizing instants when I first set eyes on the high Himalayas and to hear once more the musical clang of the oxygen cylinder rung daily at Thyangboche Monastery, summoning the monks to prayer. As in other forms of activity, I remember the small things best. Not the climb to some virgin, snow-capped summit, nor the long, hard grind up the valley floor, but the smell of mist and alpine flowers, the friendly Sherpa laughter, the burning juniper, and the sunrise hour on some high snow field.

I returned to the Navy exactly eleven months after the day we three left Camp VII, our lungs laboring avidly for the thin nourishment from the cold air. Annulu, Tom, and I were strong, full of hope, and confident that only a few hours stood between us and our summit, so deceptively close. For me those months spanned a lifetime of intolerable pain and anguish, only now blurring to my conscious recollection.

But still in my mind's eye I can see clearly the sharp wedge of Makalu as, like a moth fluttering in an airless jar, the rescuing helicopter rose slowly above the banked monsoon cloud. Turning, I took a last look. The mountain's long, unbroken southern shoulder came momentarily into view, still thousands of feet above us. My eye ran along the ridge . . . there was the upper glacier, above and to the left the bergschrund, but of the abandoned tents I could see no sign. Inevitably, my gaze lifted . . . a solitary stream of glittering snow crystals flew from the summit.

There is little doubt that the summit of Makalu can be reached without oxygen, but it is obvious that unless for some extraordinarily special purpose the risks involved are hardly worth it. A taste for adventure, however, is the very essence of human nature, and greater mountaineering will continue to provide stories of heroism, tragedy, and final achievement as long as there are mountains to be climbed or poles to be won. There are those, it is true, who are utterly out of sympathy with this type of enterprise and who question the ultimate purpose of expeditions of exploration. Opinion on this matter is dependent almost entirely on a point of view.

For my part I have no real regrets. I am fortunate to have survived at all. Naturally, I would not take the same risks again in the light of foreknowledge, but in overstepping my limitations I have discovered, like Maurice Herzog, a deeper significance of an existence hitherto unknown to me. Sir John Hunt has said that "The real measure is the success or failure of the climber to triumph, not over a lifeless mountain but over himself; the true value of the enterprise lies in the example to others of human motive and human conduct."

This I firmly believe to be true, and I hope that on Makalu, as in life, where I have made a decision, bold or imprudent, good or bad, I have had the courage to stand up and face its consequences like a man, without excuses. Sir Richard Burton eloquently states the case in his striking translation of *The Kasidah:*

> Do what thy manhood bids thee do,
>   from none but self expect applause;
> He noblest lives and noblest dies
>   who makes and keeps his self-made laws.
> All other Life is living Death,
>   a world where none but Phantoms dwell,
> A breath, a wind, a sound, a voice,
>   a tinkling of a camel-bell.

GLOSSARY

Arete:	*A narrow ridge.*
Belay:	*To secure the climber to a projection with a rope.*
Bergschrund:	*A crevasse separating the upper slopes of a glacier from the steeper slopes of ice or rock above.*
Chang:	*A beer brewed from rice.*
Col:	*Depression in a mountain chain, a pass.*
Cornice:	*Overhanging mass of snow or ice along a ridge, usually formed by the prevailing wind.*
Couloir:	*A steep gully of rock or snow.*
Crampon:	*A metal frame with spikes, fitting the sole of the boot for use on hard snow or ice.*
Cwm:	*An enclosed valley on the flank of a hill.*
Gompa:	*A Buddhist temple.*
Icefall:	*A frozen cascade of ice.*
Karabiner:	*A large metal spring-loaded clip that can be fixed to the rope or piton.*

Monsoon:	*A wind in South Asia which blows from the southwest in summer (the wet monsoon) and from the northeast in winter (the dry monsoon).*
Moraine:	*Accumulation of stones and debris brought down by the glacier.*
Pitch:	*A stretch of difficult ice or rock.*
Piton:	*Metal spike, with a ring or hole in the head, that can be driven into rock or ice. They can be used in conjunction with a karabiner to which a rope can be attached.*
Puri:	*A thick pancake of flour and water, fried and served with chilies.*
Rakshi:	*A spirit distilled usually from rice or potatoes.*
Sastrugi:	*Ridges of hard snow built up by a strong wind.*
Scree:	*Slope of small loose stones.*
Serac:	*A tower or pinnacle of ice.*
Sherpa:	*Hillmen living mostly above 7000 feet in eastern Nepal. They are Buddhists of Tibetan stock and Nepalese nationality.*
Sherpani:	*A Sherpa woman.*
Sirdar:	*The senior Sherpa or foreman.*
Stupa:	*A large hemispherical shrine of Buddhist origin.*
Tsampa:	*Flour of roasted and ground barley, staple food of Sherpas.*

Sherpas are often named after the day of the week on which they were born, as follows:

Sunday:	Nima
Monday:	Dawa
Tuesday:	Mingma
Wednesday:	Lakpa
Thursday:	Norbu
Friday:	Pasang
Saturday:	Pemba

Medical Aspects

These notes are extracted with permission, and almost in their entirety, from a paper by Dr. Michael Ward, F.R.C.S., written for the *Alpine Journal:*

At sea level the normal barometric pressure is equivalent to the weight of 760 m.m. of mercury. As the climber ascends the weight of air decreases so that at 19,000 feet it is equivalent to only 380 m.m. of mercury. The percentage of oxygen in the air, however, remains the same whatever the height, i.e., 21%.

Thus the amount of pressure driving oxygen from the lungs into the blood gets less the higher the climber ascends. It is this drop in pressure of oxygen that is the major factor in high altitude climbing. To combat this low pressure the body attempts to compensate with two major adaptive mechanisms.

In the first place more air and therefore more oxygen is passed through the lungs, and secondly there is an increase in the number of red cells and therefore in the oxygen-carrying capacity of the blood. This enables the same amount of oxygen to be carried in the blood at 19,000 feet as at sea level. However, it must be remembered that the pressure of oxygen in the blood is very much less than it is at sea level, therefore the maximum amount of oxygen that can be delivered to the tissues is very much less than at sea level and the capacity for physical exercise is reduced.

The cells that are most sensitive to oxygen lack are those of the brain and this explains why accounts of climbing at high altitude are sometimes incomplete and bizarre. It explains too the hallucinations, forgetfulness and callousness that climbers often show when high on a mountain and which is quite unlike their sea-level behaviour.

These two main adaptive processes, namely the increase in breathing rate and increase in the number of red cells, may themselves cause medical complications and illness.

Increased breathing and the dry atmosphere at extreme altitudes increase the rate of water loss from the lungs by as much as three fold. This is one reason why climbers tend to become dehydrated; other reasons are the difficulty of obtaining enough fluid from the snow because of limited fuel supplies and inefficient stoves, and the blunting of the sensation of thirst. Drying of the respiratory tract coupled with oxygen lack seems to predispose to respiratory infections, the most serious of which is pneumonia.

The increase in the number of red cells in the blood probably causes an increased liability to thrombosis. The normal ratio of red cells to plasma is 45% red cells to 55% plasma. At high altitude this ratio can change to 65% red cells to 35% plasma. The blood becomes very sticky and more difficult for the heart to push around the circulation.

Frostbite is an almost inevitable sequel of illness or accident. Warmth depends on the flow of blood around the body. In any conditions where there is "shock" the peripheral blood vessels contract and the supply of heat to the limbs is greatly reduced or cut off. The extremities, therefore, cool down to the same temperature as the surrounding air which at extreme altitudes is below freezing, and no matter how much clothing is worn, frostbite is inevitable.

Oxygen lack constricts the blood vessels of the lungs and causes a rise in pulmonary blood pressure. This increases the work on the right side of the heart and the heart enlarges. At high altitude where the climber is continuously exposed to lack of oxygen any lung condition which further impedes the absorption of oxygen is extremely dangerous. He may lose consciousness as an early symptom and signs of heart failure with pulmonary oedema may occur."

To examine the major illnesses that occurred on Makalu in the light of this knowledge is interesting and informative. To take Ward's case first; he developed a chest infection, probably at Camp VI (nearly 26,000 feet), after a period of eight days on the Makalu Col, doing work that was connected with the physiology program and that involved maximum effort. This illness manifested itself in the first place by the hallucinations he had at Camp VI followed by an inability to *descend* at a reasonable rate. He became progressively weaker and had to be dragged into a tent on the col. Here he became delirious, another manifestation of anoxia, as the brain cells are most sensitive to oxygen lack. He was treated with antibiotics and oxygen and descended forty-eight hours later with Nevison. On this descent he was occasionally delirious and felt a most extraordinary central coldness despite being fully clothed. Ward suffered frostbite of all his fingers and toes and of his nose. The explanation here probably is that the lung infection, pneumonia, strained an already strained heart and this resulted in a shutdown of the circulation. Blood and therefore heat and oxygen were not available for his peripheral vessels during the descent. His cardiac output was sufficient for lying in a sleeping bag, but not sufficient for any form of exercise. This resulted in the feeling of central coldness, frostbite, and hallucinations. An X-ray of Ward's chest at Katmandu, taken within twenty-four hours of returning by helicopter, showed an enlarged heart. Further X-rays at the London Hospital showed a gradual diminution in size of his heart until it became normal in size after three months. The frostbite took two months to clear up. On return to England he was two stone less than his normal weight of 11½ stone, and it was some months before he felt really fit.

In my case the sequence of events was probably as follows:

a clot of blood formed in my lungs at 27,400 feet, and this led to "shock," constriction of the peripheral vessels and diminution in cardiac output. This explains the coughing up of blood, collapse, and my very severe frostbite.

Sir Edmund Hillary suffered what appeared to be a transient stroke. This may have been due to a spasm of his cerebal blood vessels secondary to a transient thrombosis. Three other cases, with similar clinical features, have occurred on expeditions to the Himalayas to young and fit personnel. Two of these patients subsequently died and one recovered. Nevison considered that he had had an attack of pulmonary edema at Camp VI, as his sputum was frothy and tinged with blood; he was also very breathless at rest. An X-ray taken in America some time later showed no cardiac enlargement.

If oxygen had not been taken on Makalu, in all probability there would have been three deaths.

The precipitating factor in these three serious illnesses is not known, but Ward had just spent the winter at 19,000 feet. This had obviously taken more out of him than was generally thought at the time. In fact as a result of the winter, although the full program of work was carried out satisfactorily, the general condition of the whole wintering party was less good than that of the party coming in during the spring.

The subsequent month spent working often till after midnight at the Silver Hut tired the wintering party more than they realized. In fact 19,000 feet is too high for plainsmen to live at for long periods, and 17,000 feet or even 15,000 feet is probably the best height at which to get maximum acclimatization.

Hillary had spent one month in December and January on a round-the-world trip with the Yeti scalp after being with the expedition in the field from August to the end of November on the Yeti hunt. The scalp was flown in by him to Khumjung on January 5. He returned the same day and went back to New Zealand to organize the spring party. After he came back to the Silver Hut in March, he had to return to

Katmandu, where he spent a week to ten days clearing up the difficulties arising from the ascent of Ama Dablam. In addition to being eight years older, his physical condition in 1961 did not compare with his superb fitness in 1953.

I had spent the autumn on the Yeti hunt and then returned with the spring party. My general health appeared as good as that of any other member of the expedition, but there is little doubt that carrying a Sherpa load to 27,000 feet imposed an excessive strain on my reserves of strength.

The contrast between the physical condition of the climbers of this expedition and that of the members on the French expedition to Makalu, when all members (using oxygen) reached the summit, is quite remarkable. The same contrast was made between members of the successful Everest expedition in 1953 (using oxygen) and the prewar Everest expedition, which did not use oxygen.

The main effect of oxygen appears to be to combat physical deterioration; by using oxygen and by increasing the speed of movement on the mountains the climber can ascend more quickly, more efficiently, and more safely than he can without oxygen.

In Ward's opinion oxygen should always be taken on expeditions to Himalayan peaks as it is of lifesaving value in cases of acute pulmonary edema and pneumonia. Both of these conditions can occur below 19,000 feet. Oxygen, too, should be taken by climbers who are trying to climb peaks of over 24,000 to 25,000 feet, as it increases the climbing rate, combats deterioration, and therefore increases the margin of safety.

The following is a list of those who accompanied the expedition in Nepal, with the approximate times in the field, and their field occupations:

Yeti Party

Sir Edmund Hillary*	N.Z.	leader	10 mos.
Dr. Lawrence W. Swan	U.S.	biologist	3 mos.
Dr. Thomas O. Nevison*	U.S.	physiologist	10 mos.
Lt. Peter D. Mulgrew*	N.Z.	climber	10 mos.
Dr. Michael Gill*	N.Z.	physiologist	10 mos.
W. George Lowe*	N.Z.	photographer	3 mos.
R. Marlin Perkins	U.S.	zoologist	3 mos.
H. P. "Pat" Barcham*	N.Z.	climber	3 mos.
John W. Dienhart	U.S.	personnel	3 wks.
Desmond Doig	U.K.	reporter	9 mos.
Bhanu Bannerjee	India	reporter	9 mos.

Hut-Construction Party

Norman D. Hardie*	N.Z.	leader	3 mos.
Dr. J. S. Milledge*	U.K.	physiologist	10 mos.
Walter Romanes*	N.Z.	builder	10 mos.
Barry Bishop*	U.S.	photographer	10 mos.

Additions to Wintering Medical Party

Dr. L. G. C. E. Pugh	U.K.	leader	8 mos.
Dr. John B. West*	Austl.	physiologist	7 mos.
Michael Ward, F.R.C.S.*	U.K.	physiologist	7 mos.
Dr. S. Lahiri	India	physiologist	7 mos.
Capt. S. B. Motwani	India	physiologist	7 mos.

Additions to Makalu Party

John Harrison*	N.Z.	climber	4 mos.
Leigh Ortenberger*	U.S.	climber	4 mos.

* climbed on Makalu and/or Ama Dablam.